SONGS OF THE 1890's

PIANO • VOCAL • GUITAR

THE DECADE SERIES

ISBN 0-7935-3125-X

7777 W. Bluemound Rd. P.O. Box 13819 Milwaukee, WI 53213

SONGS OF THE 1890's

THE DECADE SERIES

The 1890's

by Elaine Schmidt

The "Gay 90's," the final decade of the Nineteenth Century, is remembered by Americans as the era of bicycles and barbershop quartets. As the country grew, adding the States of Idaho, Utah and Wyoming, the American public sought news of the world, welcomed entertainment and watched with keen interest as new inventions promised to better daily life. To the north, gold was discovered on Klondike Creek, beginning the Alaskan gold rush, while at home, cities boasted of modern wonders. The Boston subway was under construction, Chicago enjoyed the first electric, elevated railway, and *The New York Times* touted the first moving pictures seen on a public screen as, "all wonderfully real and singularly exhilarating." Thousands flocked to the spectacular Columbian Exposition in Chicago, which marked the 400th anniversary of Christopher Columbus's arrival in the New World. From Washington, D.C, presidents Benjamin Harrison, Grover Cleveland and William McKinley took their turns governing the land.

A poster celebrating "Chicago Day" at the Chicago World's Fair of 1893, officially known as the "Columbian Exposition."

American ingenuity seemed boundless in the nineties, as patents were issued for the electric stove, an electric light socket with a pull chain, the home refrigerator, and a revolutionary hookless fastener called the "zipper." Thomas Alva Edison patented the radio and the first moving picture camera.

Bicycles were all the rage in the 1890s.

Both gasoline and electric powered automobiles appeared in 1892. By decade's end New York had posted speed limits, Boston had its first public automobile garage and Cranston, R.I had hosted the nation's first auto race. For all but the very wealthy, the automobile remained a curiosity. The bicycle was the national craze and the tandem became a hot fad.

The final years of America's "Gilded Age" were not entirely innocent. The century drew to a close in an era of restlessness and sweeping change. Huge fortunes were amassed through employee exploitation and the formation of monopolies. Worker unrest and the organization of labor unions created a national climate of tension. Workers demanded the right to basic education and reasonable working hours, calling over 1,400 industrial strikes that affected over 700,000 wage-earners by mid-decade alone. Suffragettes fought for women's personal freedom, winning the right to vote in several western states, while hundreds of African Americans emigrated to Liberia, finding no place in post–Civil War America. Newspapers flourished as Americans demanded current reports from home and abroad. William Randolph Hearst, owner of the *The New York Morning Journal*, and Joseph Pulitzer, of the *World*, began a fierce competition for readership. Hearst's correspondents resorted to aggressive, inflammatory "yellow journalism." They fuelled a growing nationalistic spirit, purporting that the U.S. had a duty to protect the Western Hemisphere. The journalists helped to set the climate for the U.S. to step in when Cuba revolted against Spain. Siding with Cuba from the start, America declared war on Spain in April of 1898. Col. Theodore Roosevelt and his all-volunteer Rough Riders defeated the Spanish forces in less than 5 months. The brief Spanish-American War cost 5,462 American lives, 90% of which were lost to disease.

One of the world's first skyscrapers was the Guaranty Building in Buffalo, 1894.

Teddy Roosevelt and his "roughriders" in the Spanish-American war.

The decade held many other hardships. Economic woes escalated until the stock market crashed in 1893. Unemployed and homeless men from all corners of the country marched on Washington D.C. in an attempt to force Congress to help them. Although unsuccessful, they drew tremendous public support. The Oklahoma Territory was formed and opened to white homesteaders, stripping Indians of millions of acres. The Metropolitan Opera House was almost totally destroyed in a 1892 fire. The cities of Boston, Minneapolis, Chicago and Milwaukee also suffered catastrophic fires. Cyclones wiped two Kansas towns from the map, devastated Savannah, reduced huge sections of St. Louis to ruins, and leveled much of the Louisiana Gulf Coast. Flames, swept along by a cyclone, killed 500 while devastating Hinkley, Minnesota and 18 neighboring towns. A Yellow Fever epidemic decimated Brunswick, Georgia.

All the while, a steady flow of hopeful foreigners was inexorably changing the look and feel of the country. Over the course of the decade, some 3,687,000 immigrants would flood American shores. In 1892 an immigration processing facility was opened at New York's Ellis Island, followed by the creation of the Bureau of Immigration two years later. The demographics of New York City in 1890 revealed the true extent of the American "melting pot." The city was home to half as many Italians as Naples Italy, as many Germans as Hamburg Germany, twice as many Irish as Dublin and two and one-half times as many Jews as Warsaw.

Americans were hungry for the arts. American painter Mary Cassatt thrived among the French Impressionists while Winslow Homer painted his famous "Coast in Winter." Soprano Nellie Melba's Metropolitan Opera debut was such a hit that she found a type of toast and a peach dessert named in her honor. Funded by Andrew Carnegie, a grand Music Hall was built in New York City. Opening night featured an all Tchaikovsky concert conducted by the composer himself. The structure would later be renamed Carnegie Hall. Journalist Nellie Bly returned from a trip around the world — the first ever for a woman alone. It was during the '90s that innovative architect Frank Lloyd Wright began his independent design commissions.

New York harbor, the arrival point for millions of immigrants from Europe.

William Jennings Bryan (left) and his wife (right) greet voters in the presidential campaign of 1896. Bryan lost to McKinley.

"California, the Cornucopia of the World" proclaims this advertisement, aimed at the millions of immigrants to the U.S.

The country's literary life thrived with the publication of Mark Twain's *The Tragedy of Pudd'nhead Wilson* and *Joan of Arc*. Walt Whitman's final edition of *Leaves of Grass*, Henry James' *The Turn of the Screw* appeared along with Stephen Crane's *The Red Badge of Courage*. Rudyard Kipling released *The Jungle Book* and *Captains Courageous*, while Anthony Hope's *The Prisoner of Zenda* arrived. From Britain came Sir Arthur Conan Doyle's *The Adventures of Sherlock Holmes* and Robert Louis Stevenson's *The Strange Case of Dr. Jekyll and Mr. Hyde*. In 1890, Jacob A. Riis published *How the Other Half Lives*, which exposed the squalor and hopelessness of tenement life and began a movement of reform. The "Yellow Kid" and "The Katzenjammer Kids" began a cartoon craze and Francis Bellamy published his "Pledge of Allegiance to the Flag."

In theater, lyric productions began to divide into operetta, musical comedy and revue, anticipating future trends. European imports thrived on American stages. Victor Herbert, a cellist and conductor who had emigrated from Dublin, tried his hand at operettas. His successful *The Wizard of the Nile* (1895), *The Serenade* (1897), and *The Fortune Teller* (1898), with its familiar "Gypsy Love Song", established him as a serious contender in the world of comic opera. From America's "March King," John Philip Sousa, came *El Capitan* (1896), the most successful of his ten comic operas. *Robin Hood* (1891) featured the song "Oh Promise Me," to which countless wedding vows have since been exchanged. "After the Ball," interpolated into *A Trip to Chinatown* (1891), became one of the most successful songs of all time when Sousa's band played it daily at the Columbian Exhibition. "The Bowery," Chinatown's biggest number, was much of the reason for the show's success. *Sinbad* (1892) created a lavish spectacle while the trendy, British *A Gaiety Girl* (1894) set fashion trends on both sides of the Atlantic. *The Belle of New York* (1897) trod a new path, first finding success in New York and then moving to London for a run of 697 performances. From the touring company of *A Parlor Match* came "The Man Who Broke the Bank at Monte Carlo." From the 1892 remount of *The Black Crook* came "Ta Ra Ra Boom De Ay." "Musetta's Waltz" from Puccini's opera *La Bohème*, and Dvorak's "Humoresque" also became popular favorites. In 1891, a 13 year-old boy made an unremarkable stage debut. In the coming years he would become a fixture in the American musical theater. His name was George M. Cohan.

Throughout the country, sheet music was selling by the ream. Entertainment for most families meant an evening gathered around the parlor piano. Popular songs of the day reflected every facet of American culture, including its ethnic diversity and religious beliefs, as well as fads and trends. "The Rosary" (1898) remained America's most popular song for 25 years. Irish songs, like "My Wild Irish Rose," (1899) "Who Threw the Overalls in Mistress Murphy's Chowder," (1899) "Sweet Rosie O'Grady," (1896) were particular favorites. Italian hearts were touched by "O Sole Mio." American nationalism was roused by "America the Beautiful" (1898) and John Philip Sousa's "The Stars and Stripes Forever" (1896), which

Tastes for ornate fashions prevailed in the decade.

A Hot Time in the Old Town
Words by Joe Hayden
Written by Theo. A. Metz
Break the News to Mother
Chas. K. Harris
Hello ma Baby
By Howard & Emerson
I Don't Want to Play in Your Yard
Music by H. W. Petrie
Words by Philip Wingate
Petrie Music Company
Chicago, Ill.
In the Baggage Coach Ahead
Song and Refrain
Written & Composed by Gussie L. Davis
Hearts and Flowers
Coeurs et Fleurs
A New Flower Song
by Theo. M. Tobani
Carl Fischer
Kentucky Babe
A Plantation Lullaby
Words by Richard Henry Buck
Music by Adam Geibel
White-Smith Music Publishing Co.
Boston New York Chicago
After the Ball
Sung by J. Aldrich Libbey
Chas. K. Harris
Song for Baritone or Bass Voice
Asleep in the Deep
Words by A. J. Lamb
Music by H. W. Petrie

made a fortune for Sousa. Folk songs, which rarely become commercial successes, broke the rules with "The Cat Came Back," "Red River Valley," and "She'll Be Comin' Round the Mountain."

Sentimental ballads were particular favorites during the 90's. Extolling the virtues of motherhood and family, they were intended to bring a tear to the eye. They told heartbreaking tales of fallen women, soldiers far from home, or tragic deaths. Written about the Civil War, "Break the News to Mother" (1897) took on new meaning during the Spanish-American War. "She May Have Seen Better Days" (1894) and "She Is More to Be Pitied than Censured," spoke of fallen women. "Just Tell Them That You Saw Me" (1895) recounted a tragic love affair.

"Just tell them that you saw me" quickly became a national catch phrase, even appearing on printed lapel badges. Other successful ballads included "The Sweetest Story Ever Told," "Those Wedding Bells Shall Not Ring Out" (1896), and "When You Were Sweet Sixteen." Instrumental selections also caught the public ear. "Hearts and Flowers" was heard on piano during countless tragic or sentimental sequences in silent films. Scott Joplin's engaging "Maple Leaf Rag" (1899) was named for the Maple Leaf Club in Sedalia Missouri.

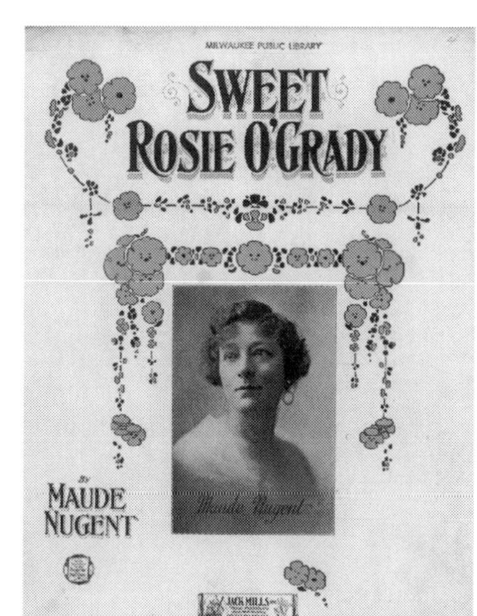

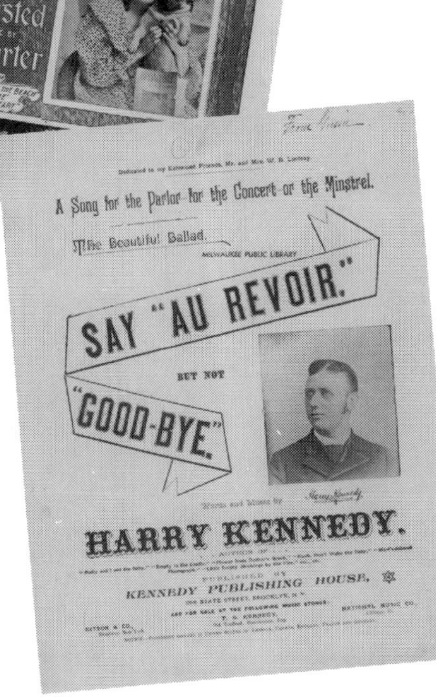

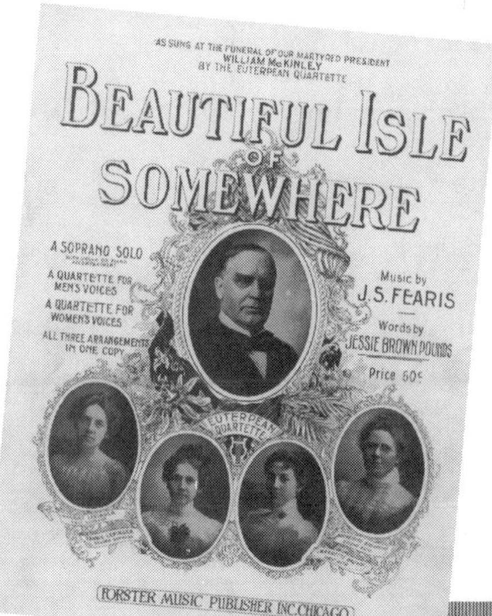

Other songs simply touched the nation. "Asleep in the Deep," a low voice favorite, inspired a bevy of sea songs. "Daisy Bell" (A Bicycle Built for Two) emerged from the bicycle craze sweeping the country. "I've Been Working on the Railroad," the oldest and most famous of the railroad songs, became a favorite of railway crews. "Hello! Ma Baby," was one of the first telephone songs, as well as a big ragtime — cakewalk hit. Paul Dresser remembered his Indiana home with "On The Banks of the Wabash, Far Away." The song sold a million copies in its first year and was later adopted as the Indiana state song. "The Sidewalks of Old New York" (East Side West Side) became the unofficial song of the

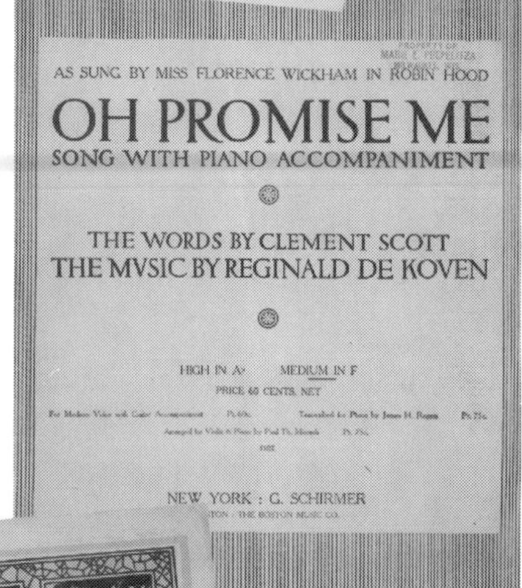

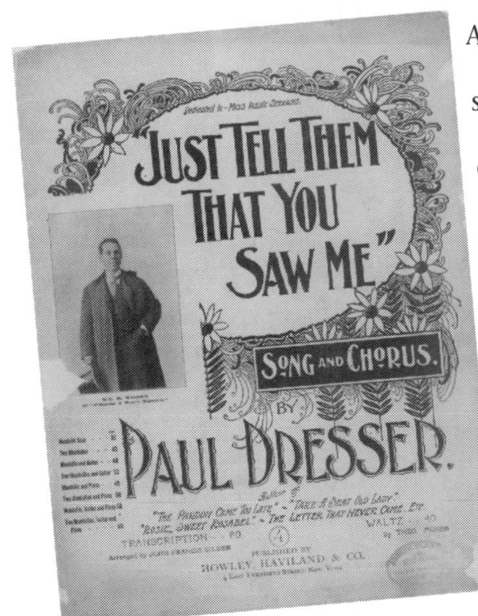

A Tiller-Steered Motor Wagon, the automobile driven in America's first known car race, Thanksgiving Day, 1895 in Chicago.

city of New York. First heard in minstrel shows, "A Hot Time in the Old Town Tonight," became a favorite with Teddy Roosevelt and the Rough Riders.

By the end of the 90's, American life moved at a ever accelerating pace. The automobile and an endless stream of new inventions had created a new world. For better or worse, the country was changing. One of the reassuring constants that would remain a part of the country's culture for years to come, was a love and hunger for American songs. Over the coming years, popular songs would continue to express the fads, morals hopes and dreams of the growing nation.

By 1899 women too had begun to drive.

AFTER THE BALL

Words and Music by
CHAS. K. HARRIS

D7
Gm
Why are you sin - gle; why live a - lone?............
There came my sweet - - heart, my love, my own–............
She tried to tell me, tried to ex - plain;........
Eb
Edim7
Bb
C7
F7
Bb
Have you no ba - - - bies; have you no home?... ....
'I wish some wa - - - ter; leave me a - lone'.........
I would not list - en, plead - - ings were vain,..........
Gm
D7
Eb
F7
Bb
"I had a sweet - heart, years, years a - go;..........
When I re - turned dear there stood a man,..........
One day a let - - - ter came from that man,..........

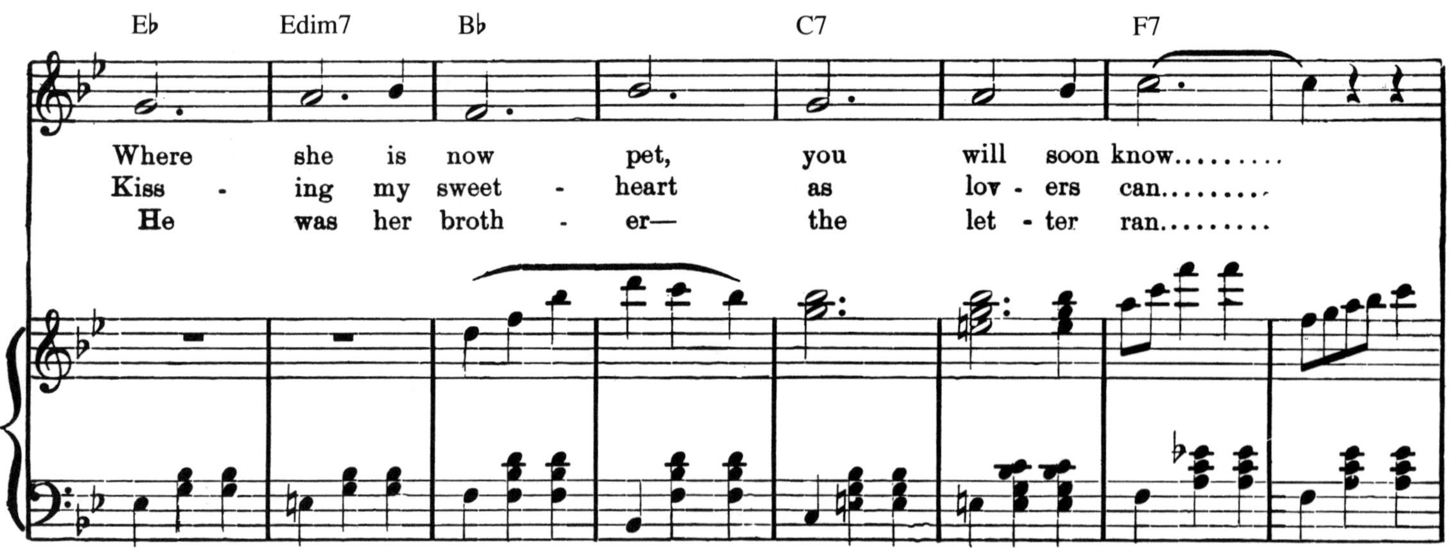
Eb
Edim7
Bb
C7
F7
Where she is now pet, you will soon know.........
Kiss - ing my sweet - heart as lov - ers can.........
He was her broth - er— the let - ter ran.........

Bb
D7
Gm
List to the sto - ry, I'll tell it all,..........
Down fell the glass pet, brok - - en, that's all,..........
That's why I'm lone - ly, no home at all;..........
p

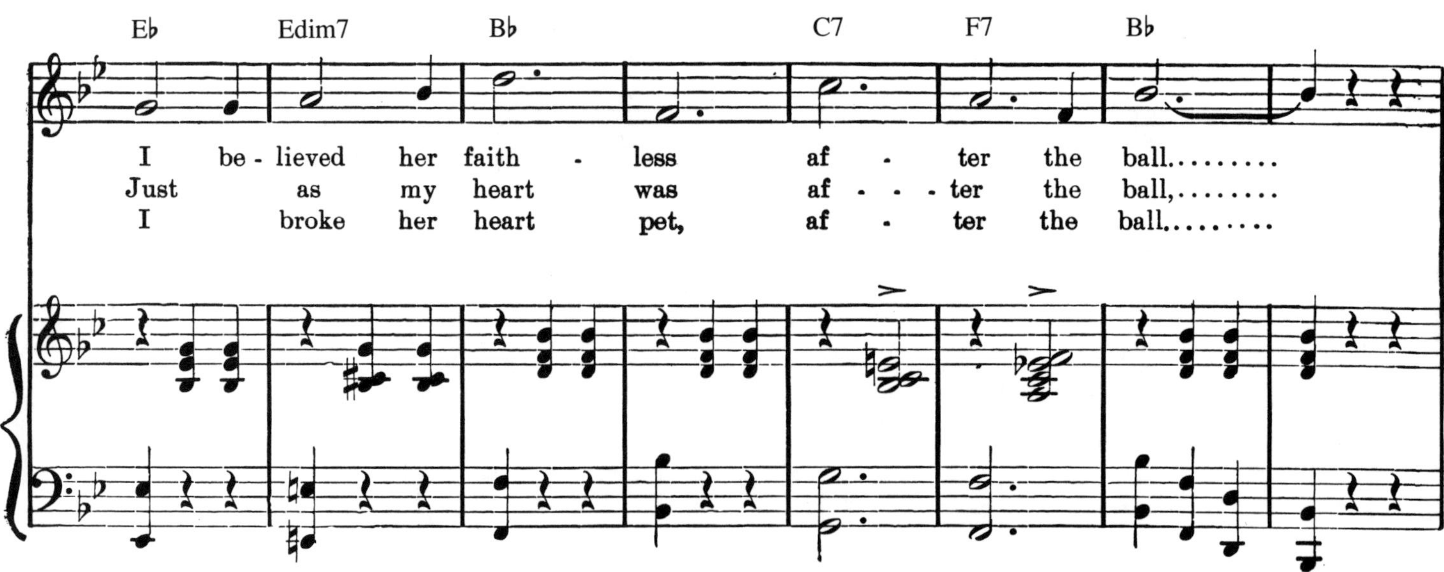
Eb
Edim7
Bb
C7
F7
Bb
I be - lieved her faith - less af - ter the ball.........
Just as my heart was af - - - ter the ball,........
I broke her heart pet, af - ter the ball.........

F7
After the ball is o - - ver, after the break of morn— After the dan - cers'
Fdim7 F7 Bb
leav - ing; af- ter the stars are gone;........ Many a heart is ach - ing,
tr
G7 C C7 F7 Bb C7 F7
if you could read them all;...... Ma- ny the hopes that have van - ished af - - ter the
Bb F7 Bb C7 F7 Bb D. S.
ball..... ...
f
D.S.

AMERICA THE BEAUTIFUL

Words by KATHERINE LEE BATES
Music by SAMUEL WARD

Additional Lyrics

3. O beautiful for heroes proved
In liberating strife
Who more than self their country loved
And mercy more than life!
America! America!
May God thy gold refine
'Til all success be nobleness
And every gain divine.

4. O beautiful for patriot dream
That sees beyond the years
Thine alabaster cities gleam
Undimmed by human tears
America! America!
God shed His grace on thee
And crown thy good with brotherhood
From sea to shining sea.

ASLEEP IN THE DEEP

Words by ARTHUR J. LAMB
Music by H. W. PETRIE

B♭
F
E7
Am
Hark! while the light-house bell's sol - emn cry
Rings o'er the sul - len tide.........
Save where the wreck- age hath strewn the shore,
Peace-ful the sun doth shine........
C7
F
There on the deck see two lov - ers stand,
Heart to heart- beat-ing and hand in hand, Tho'
But when the wild rag - ing storm did cease,
Un - der the bil - lows two hearts found peace, No
E7
Am
E7
Am
F♯dim7
C/G
G7
C
death be near, she knows no fear,
While at her side is one of all most dear.
more to part, no more of pain,
The bell may now toll its warn- ing in vain.

F
REFRAIN.
C7
Loud - - ly the bell.......... in the old.......... tow - er rings,.........

F
C7
Bid - - ding us list.......... to the warn - - ing it brings.........

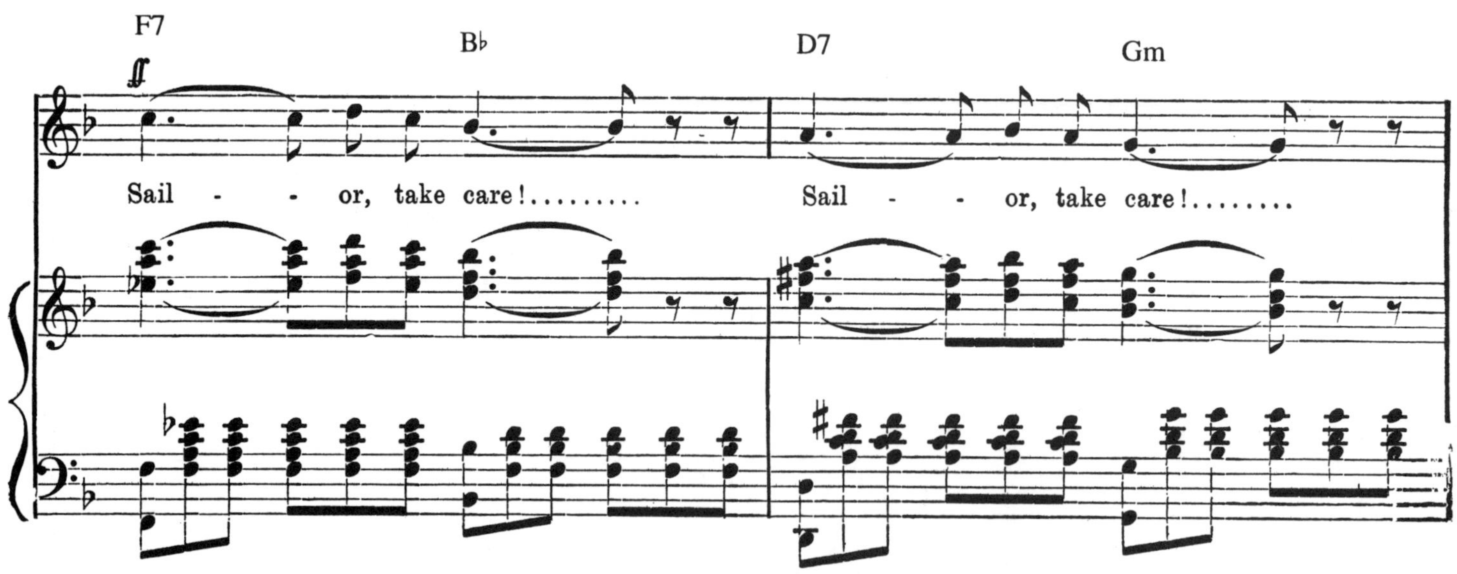
F7
B♭
D7
Gm
Sail - - or, take care!.........
Sail - - or, take care!........

F
C7
F
Dan - - ger ls near.......... thee, Be - ware! Be - - ware..........
B♭
F
Gm7
A
Be - - - - - ware! Be - - - - - - - ware!
no chord
ad lib.
F/C
C7
F
Man- y brave hearts are a - sleep in the deep, So be- ware! be - - ware!........
A7
Dm
Gm
F/C
C7
F
Man - y brave hearts are a - sleep in the deep, So be - ware! be - - ware!......

THE BAND PLAYED ON

Words by JOHN F. PALMER
Music by CHARLES B. WARD

Bm
pay day came a - round each week they greased the floor with wax. And
Ca - sey was the fa - vor - ite and he that ran the ball. Of
thank'd them ver - y kind - ly for the fa vors they had shown. Then he'd
E7
A
danced with noise and vig - or at the ball, Each
kiss - ing and love - mak - ing did his share, At
waltz once with the girl that he loved best. Most
F♯m
Bm
C♯7
F♯m
Sat - ur - day you'd see them dressed up in Sun - day clothes, Each
twelve o - clock ex - act - ly they all would fall in line, Then
all the friends are mar - ried that Ca - sey used to know, And

B7
E B7 E7 A
lad would have his sweet-heart by his side. When Ca - sey led the
march down to the din - ing hall and eat. But Ca - sey would not
Ca - sey too has tak - en him a wife. The blond he used to
Bm
E7
first grand march they all would fall in line, Be - hind the man who
join them al - though ev'-ry thing was fine, But he stayed up - stairs and
waltz and glide with on the ball room floor, Is hap - py miss - is
A
E B7/E E7
was their joy and pride, For
ex - er - cise his feet, For
Ca - sey now for life, For
CHORUS.
Valse
A
E7
Ca - sey would waltz with a straw-ber - ry blonde, And the Band played

A
on, He'd glide cross the floor with the girl he a - dor'd, and the Band
tr
tr
E7 A7 D
played on, But his brain was so load-ed it near - ly ex - plod - ed, The
F♯7 Bm D♯dim7 A/E
poor girl would shake with a - larm. He'd ne'er leave the girl with the straw-ber-ry
F♯m B7 E7 1.A 2.A
curls, And the Band played on.
f

THE BOWERY

Words by CHAS. H. HOYT
Music by PERCY GAUNT
Tempo di Valse.
Fm
Eb
Bb7
Eb
f
p
f
1. Oh! the
2. I had
3. I went
4. I went
5. I went
6. I struck a
Bb7
night that I struck New York, I went out for a
walk'd but a block or two, When up came a fel - low and
in - to an auc - tion store, I nev - er saw a - ny
in - to a con - cert hall, I did - n't have a good
in - to a bar - ber shop, He talk'd till I thought he would
place that they called a "dive," I was in luck to get

Eb
Cm
Bb 7
qui - et walk; Folks who are "on to" the ci - ty say,
me he knew; Then a po - lice - man came walk - ing by,
thieves be - fore; First he sold me a pair of socks,
time at all; Just the min - ute that I sat down
nev - er stop; I, cut it short, he mis - un - der - stood,
out a - live; When the po - lice - man heard my woes,
Eb
Bet - ter by far that I took Broad - way; But I was
Chased him a - way, and I ask'd him why? "Was - n't he
Then said he, "how much for the box?" Some - one said
Girls be - gan sing - ing, "New Coon in Town," I got up
Clipp'd down my hair just as close as he could; He shaved with a
Saw my black eyes and my bat - tered nose, "You've been held
Bb 7
out to en - joy the sights, There was the Bow - 'ry a
pull - ing your leg," said he; Said I "He nev - er laid
"two dol - lars!" I said "three!" He emp - tied the box and gave
mad and spoke out free, "Some - bo dy put that man
ra - zor that scratch'd like a pin, Took off my whis - kers and
up!" said the "cop - - per" fly! "No, sir! but I've been knock'd

Eb
Cm
Bb 7
blaze with lights; I . . . . . had one of the dev - il's own
hands on me!" "Get off the Bow - 'ry you Yep!" said
it to me,— "I sold you the box, not the socks," said
out," said she; A man called a bounc - er at - tend - ed to
most of my chin; That was the worst scrape I ev - er got
down!" said I; Then . . . . he laughed, tho' I could - 'nt see
Eb
nights! I'll nev - er go there a - - ny more! . . . .
he, I'll nev - er go there a - - ny more! . . . .
he, I'll nev - er go there a - - ny more! . . . .
me, I'll nev - er go there a - - ny more! . . . .
in, I'll nev - er go there a - - ny more! . . . .
why! I'll nev - er go there a - - ny more! . . . .
CHORUS.
Bb 7
The Bow - - - - - 'ry, the Bow - - - - - - 'ry! They
mf

Cm
Bb7
Eb
say such things, and they do strange things on the Bow - - - -
'ry! The Bow - - - - 'ry! I'll nev - er go there a - ny
Bb7
Eb
D. C.
more! . . . . ,
(After last verse.)
D. C.
f
cresc.
Eb
Tacet
Bb7
Eb
ff

BREAK THE NEWS TO MOTHER

Words and Music by
CHAS. K. HARRIS

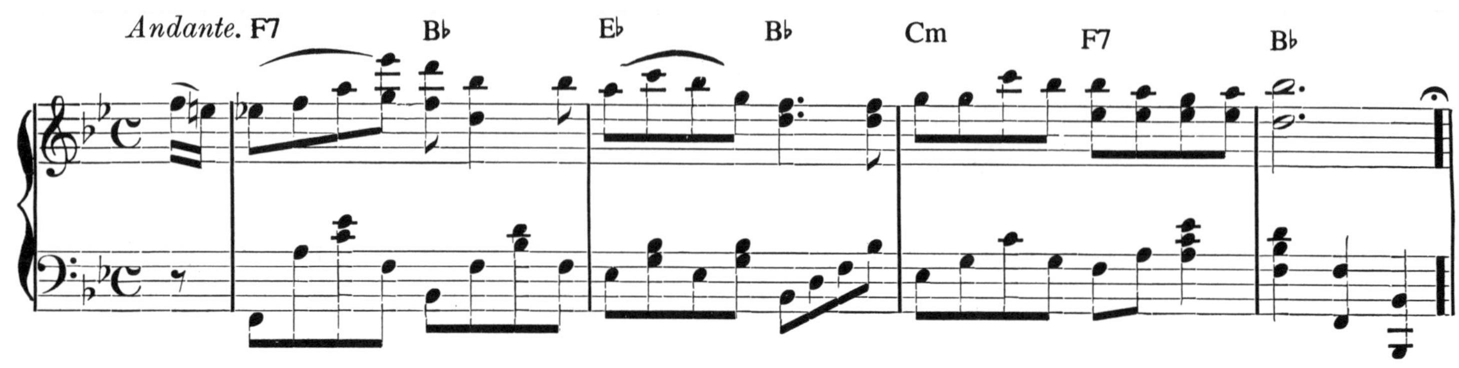

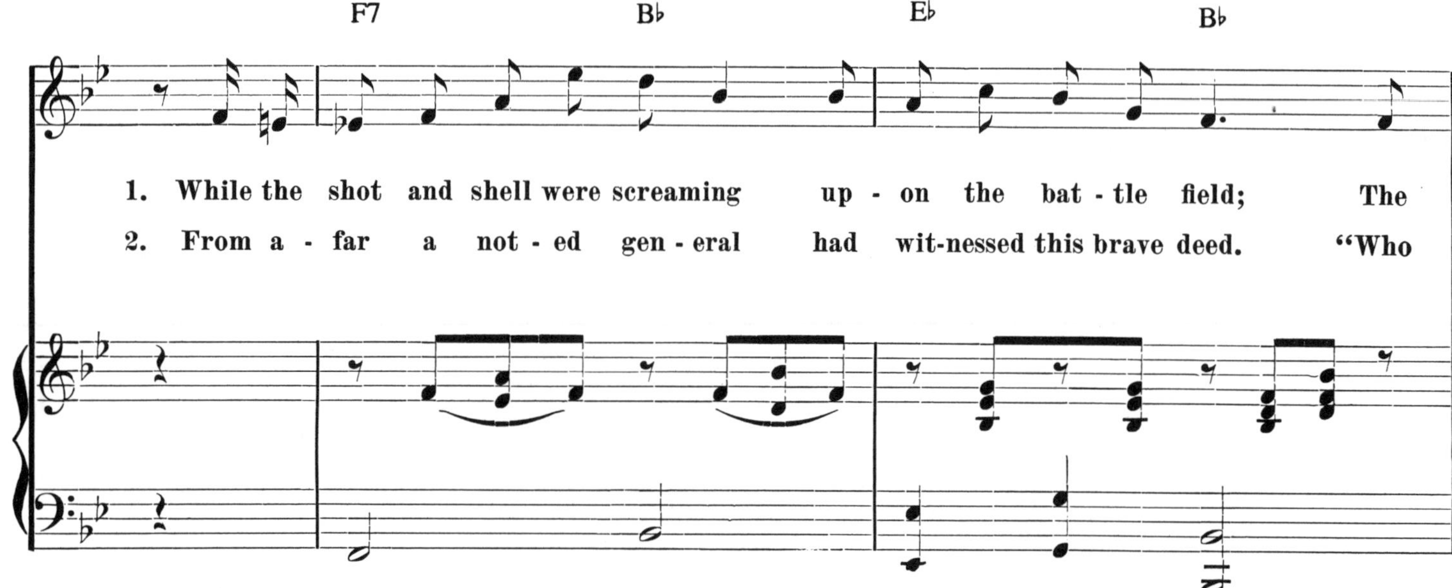

F7
B♭
C7
F7
boys in blue were fight - ing their no - ble flag to shield; Came a
saved our flag? speak up lads; 'twas no - ble, brave, in - deed!" There he
B♭
E♭
B♭
cry from their brave cap - tain, "Look, boys! our flag is down; Who'll
lies, sir," said the cap - tain, "he's sink - ing ver - y fast;" Then
Cm
F7
B♭
Gm
D7
vol - un - teer to save it from dis - grace?" "I will," a young voice shout - ed, "I'll
slow - ly turned a - way to hide a tear. The gen - eral in a mo - ment, knelt

Gm
C
F7
bring it back, or die;" Then sprang in - to the thick-est of the fray; Saved the
down be - side the boy; Then gave a cry that touch'd all hearts that day. "It's my
B♭
E♭
B♭
flag but gave his young life; all for his coun - try's sake. They
son, my brave, young he - ro; I thought you safe at home." "For-
Cm
F7
B♭
brought him back and soft - ly heard him say:
give me, fath - er. for I ran a - way."

CHORUS.
Very slow.
B♭ G7 Cm F7 B♭
Just break the news to moth - er, She knows how dear I love her, And
E♭ B♭ C7 F7
tell her not to wait for me, For I'm not com - ing home; Just
rit.
B♭ G7 Cm F7 B♭
say there is no oth - er Can take the place of moth - er; Then
E♭ B♭ G♭7 B♭/F F7 B♭
kiss her dear, sweet lips for me, And break the news to her."
D.C.

BEAUTIFUL ISLE OF SOMEWHERE

Words by MRS. JESSIE BROWN POUNDS
Music by J. S. FEARIS

REFRAIN
Eb7 Ab Fm Bb7 Eb Eb7
Some - where, Some - where, Beau - ti - ful Isle of Some - where!
Ab Eb Ab7 Db Ab/Eb rit. Eb7 Ab
Land of the true, where we live a-new Beau-ti-ful Isle of Some-where!
rit.
Ab Eb7sus Eb7 Db/Ab Ab
2. Some-where the day is long - er, Somewhere the task is done;
3. Some-where the load is lift ed, Close by an o - pen gate;

E♭
B♭
B♭7
E♭
Some-where the heart is strong-er, Some-where the guer don - won.
Some-where the clouds are rift - ed, Some-where the an - gels wait.
E♭7
REFRAIN
A♭
Fm
B♭7
E♭
E♭7
rit.
Some - where, Some - where, Beau - ti - ful Isle of Some where!
rit.
A♭
E♭
A♭7
D♭
A♭/E♭
rit.
E♭7
A♭
D.S.
Land of the true, where we live a - new Beau-ti-ful Isle of Some-where!
rit.
D.S.

COAX ME

Words by ANDREW STERLING
Music by HARRY Von TILZER

C7
F
like a tur - tle dove he's sweet - ly coo - ing; On those
noise that sound - ed just like some one kiss - ing; And a
E♭
C7
F7
B♭
ru - by lips I'd like to press a kiss Lize,— Just one or
ten - der voice said "give me just one more, Lize,— That one I
F7
B♭
E♭
C7
F7
two,— per-haps a few;— Can't I take you in my arms, A mo - ment's
had,— made me so glad,— Don't you think you bet - ter make it three or
B♭
Bdim
C7
F7
poco rall.
bliss, Lize, Just be - cause you are the girl I wants to wed; But she said:
four, Lize, And I'll pay them back to you the day we wed;" But she said:
rall.

Slowly.
CHORUS
p-f
B♭
G7
C7
"Coax me, go on and coax me,
F7
E7/E♭
B♭/D
Bdim
F7
B♭
G7
If you love me mad - ly, want me bad - ly, Coax me; go on and
C7
F7
coax me, I'll be your toot - sie, woot - sie, If you'll
C7
F7
B♭
B♭dim
1.
Coax me." "But you must
C7
F7
B♭
2.
Coax me."

THE CAT CAME BACK

Words and Music by
HARRY S. MILLER

Tempo Schottisch.

Author of "I'm 17 to-day," "Not on your Life, says Dolan," etc., etc.

1. Dar was ole Mis - ter John - son, he had troub - le of his own,
2. De cat did hab some com - pa - ny one night out in de yard,

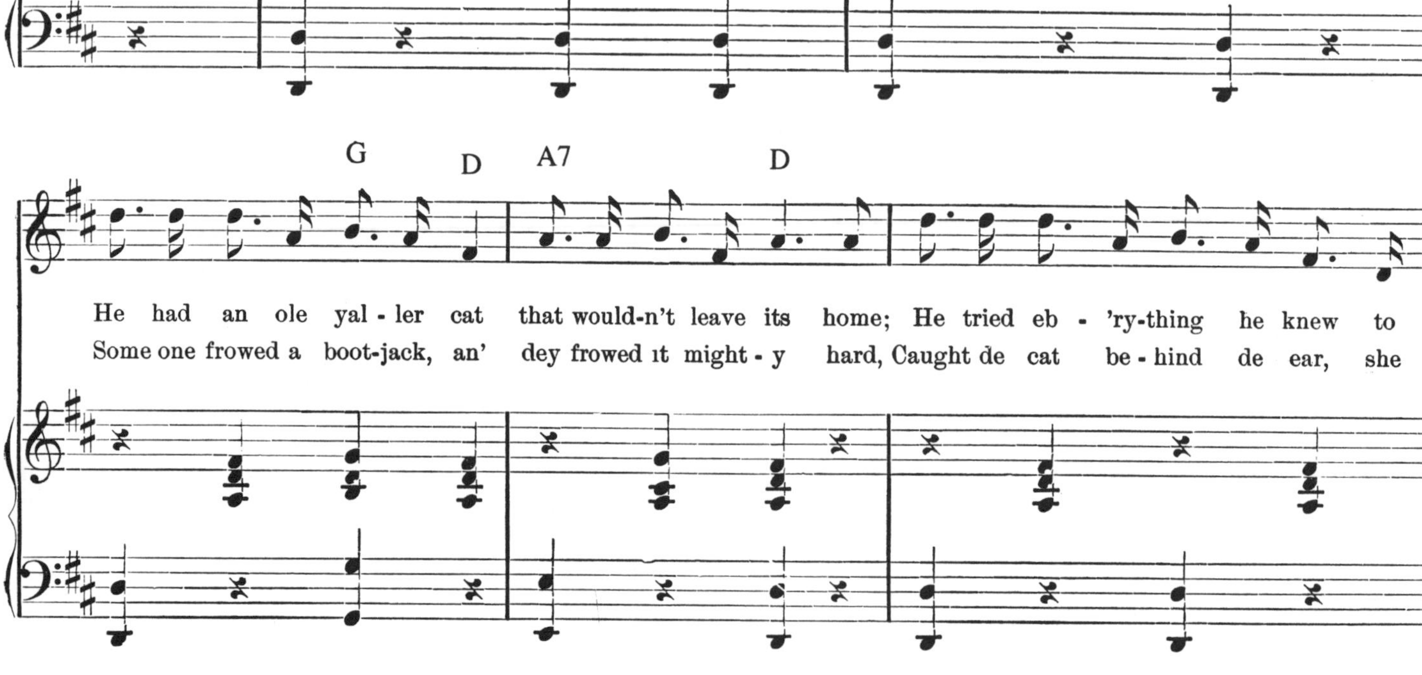

Bm
F♯
Bm
F♯
keep de cat a - way, E - ben send it to the preach - er an he tole it for to stay,
thought it rath - er slight, When a - long dar comes a brick - bat an' it knocked it out ob sight.
CHORUS.
D
A7
D
G
D
But the cat came back, could - n't stay no long - er, Yes, the
A7
D
B♭
D
A7
D
cat came back the ver - y next day, The cat came back,
G
D
Gm
D
A7
D
thought he was a gon - er, But the cat came back for it would - n't stay a - way.

DAISY BELL

Words and Music by
HARRY DACRE

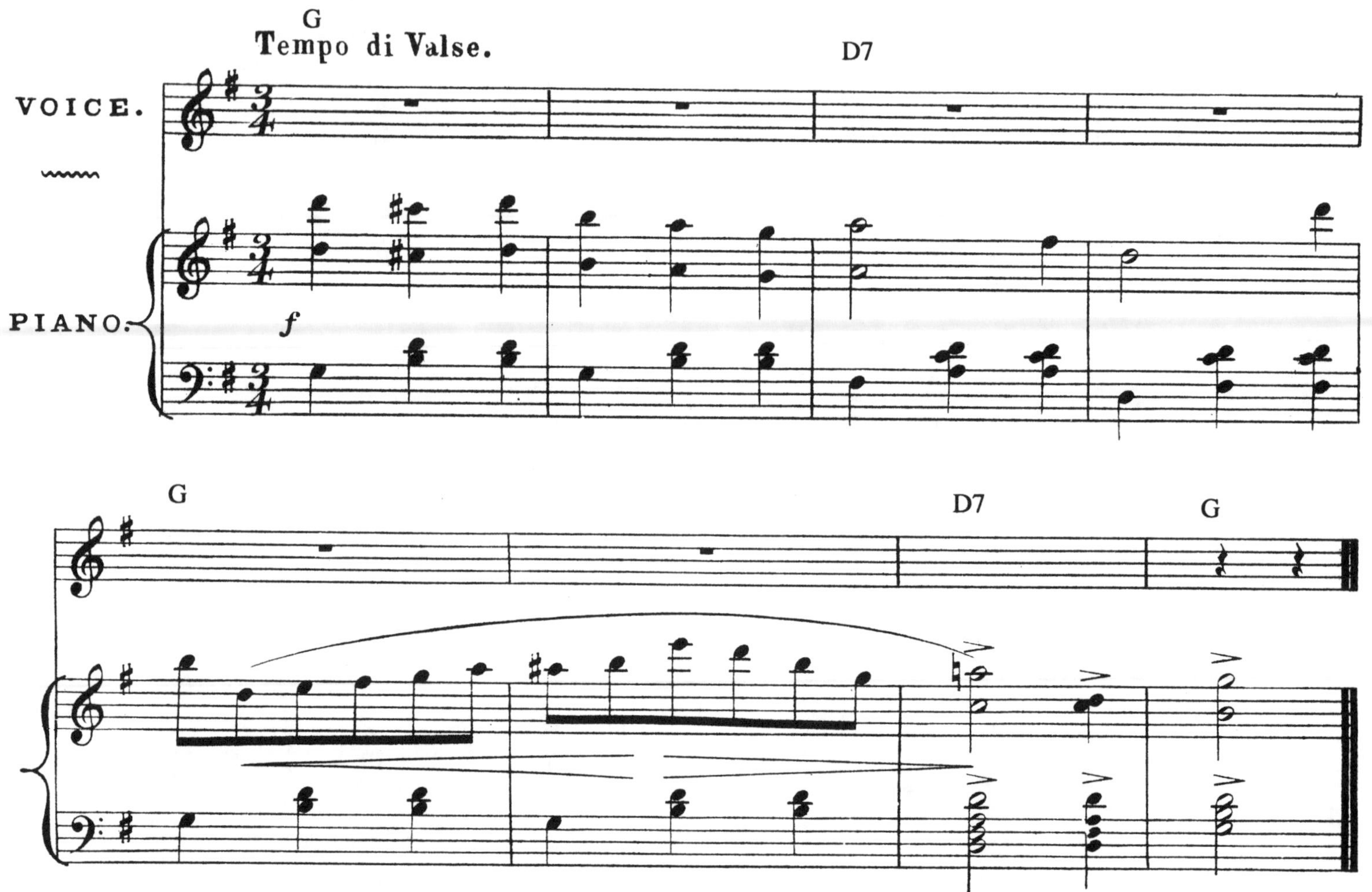

Key G.
There is a flow-er with-in my heart, Dai - - - - sy,
Dai - - - - sy!
Planted one day by a glanc - ing dart,
Planted by Dai - - sy Bell! . . . . . .
Whe-ther she loves me or loves me not,
Sometimes it's hard to tell; . . . . . .
Yet I am long-ing to share the lot
Of Beauti - ful Dai - - sy Bell! . . . . .
mf
rit.

CHORUS. (a little faster.)
G
C
G
Dai - - - sy, Dai - - - sy, Give me your an-swer, do! . . . . . .
mf
D7
G
Em
A7
D
I'm half cra - - - zy, All for the love of you! . . . . . It
D7
G
Em
C
G
D7
won't be a styl - - ish mar-riage, . . I can't af-ford a car-riage, . . But
G
D7
G
D7
G
D7
G
you'll look sweet on the seat Of a bi-cy-cle built for two! . . . . .
G
D7
G
D7
G
f

Key G.
G
D7
We will go "tan-dem" as man and wife, Dai-----sy,
I will stand by you in "wheel" or woe, Dai-----sy,
mf
G
D7
Dai-----sy! "Ped'ling" a-way down the road of life,
Dai-----sy! You'll be the bell(e) which I'll ring, you know!
G
D7
G
Em
B7
I and my Dai---sy Bell!..... When the road's dark we can
Sweet lit-tle Dai---sy Bell!..... You'll take the "lead" in each
Em
D7
G
Em
both des-pise P'liceman and "lamps" as well;...... There are "bright
"trip" we take, Then if I don't do well;..... I will per-
B7
Em
Key D.t.
A7
f. Key G.
rit.
D7
lights" in the daz-zling eyes Of beau-ti-ful Dai-sy Bell!.....
mit you to use the break, My beau-ti-ful Dai--sy Bell!.....
rit.

CHORUS. (a little faster.)
G
C
G
Dai - - - sy, Dai - - - sy, Give me your an-swer, do! . . . . . .
mf
D7
G
Em
A7
D
I'm half cra - - - zy, All for the love of you! . . . . . It
D7
G
Em
C
G
D7
won't be a styl - - ish mar-riage, . . I can't af-ford a car-riage, . . But
G
D7
G
D7
G
D7
G
you'll look sweet on the seat Of a bi-cy-cle built for two! . . . . .
G
D7
G
D7
G
f

GYPSY LOVE SONG

Words by HARRY B. SMITH
Music by VICTOR HERBERT

Baritone and Mezzo Bass in A.

F C7/F F6 F+ F
bird___ that nests in the green-wood tree___ But sighs___ to greet you and
wild rose fades in the leaf - y shades___ Its ghost___ will find you and
C7/F Fb5 F F+ F F+ F6
kiss you, All the vi - o - lets yearn, yearn for your safe re - turn, But
haunt you, All the friends say come, come to your wood-land home, And
B7 B7b5 ten. E7 rit. E7sus E7
most of all___ I miss you.___
most of all___ I want you.___
rit.
CHORUS. a tempo.
A D A B7 E7
Slum - ber on my lit-tle gypsy sweetheart, Dream of the field and the
a tempo.
dolcissimo.

D/A
A
D
A
grove,
Can you hear me, hear me in that dreamland
B7
E7
D/A
A
C#7
Where your fan - cies rove?
Slum - ber on, my
F#7
B7
E7sus
rit
E7
lit-tle gyp-sy sweet - heart, Wild lit-tle wood - land dove,
rit
A
D
A
F7
rit.
A/E
E7
A
Can you hear the song that tells you All my heart's true love?
molto rit.

HEARTS AND FLOWERS

Words by MARY D. BRINE
Music by THEO. MOSES-TOBANI

Cm
G7
Un Poco Agitato.
Cm
And the sun - - beams lov - - ing-ly,
Till it yields for you a-lone,
Un Poco Agitato.
mf
G/D
D7
G
Kiss sweet Mar - gue-rite for me.
Won - d'rous fra - - grance all your own.
rall.
Eb
Ebdim7
Eb
Bb7
Ebdim7
Eb
Tempo Imo
Kiss my lit - tle la - - dy sweet,
And its sweet - est flow - ers shall grow,
Tempo Imo
f
mf

Cm Ab Eb
Eb/Bb
Bb7 Eb
rall.
Ab
Cm
Blue eyed gen - tle Mar - - gue-rite!
For my Mar - gue - rite I know!
ff
mf
p
Ab7
G
D. S.
Cm Fm
Bb7 Eb
Bb7
Eb
3. Blush-es deep-en in her cheek, Ere the shy red lips can speak,
f
p
D. S.
Cm Ab
C7 Fm
Eb/Bb
Bb7 Eb
"Ah! but what if weeds should grow, Mongst the flow-ers you bid me sow?"

Un Poco Agitato.
Cm
G7
Cm
Love will pluck them out, I cry,
Un Poco Agitato.
mf
G/D
D7
G
Trust me, Mar - gue - rite so shy,
rall.
Tempo I.
Eb
Ebdim7
Eb
Bb7
Ebdim7
Eb
Let my heart your gar - den be
Tempo I.
f
mf
Cm
Ab
Eb
Eb/Bb
Bb7
Eb
Give the seeds of love to me.
ff

HELLO! MA BABY

By HOWARD and EMERSON

nev - er seen my hon - ey but she's mine, all right; So
sat - is - fied be - cause I'se got my babe's ad - dress, Here
take my tip, an' leave this gal a - lone............
past - ed in the lin - ing of my hat............
F
Ev - 'ry sin - gle morn - ing, you will hear me yell, "Hey
I am might - y scared, 'cause if the wires get crossed, 'Twill
D7
Cen - tral! fix me up a - long the line.".......... He con -
sep - a - rate me from ma ba - by mine,. .... Then some
Gm D7 Gm

C7
F
D7
-nects me with ma hon - ey, then I rings the bell, And
oth - er man will win her, and my game is lost, And
G7
C7
this is what I say to ba - by mine,............
so each day I shout a - long the line,............
F
CHORUS.
"Hel - lo! ma ba - by, Hel - lo! ma hon - ey,
G7
C7
Hel - lo! ma rag - time gal,............ Send me a kiss by

F
E7
F
F♯dim7
C7
wire,............
Ba - by my heart's on fire!............
F
G7
If you re - fuse me, Hon - ey, you'll lose me, Then you'll be left a -
C7
- lone; oh, ba - by, Tel - e - phone and tell me I'se your
1
F
C7
F
C
2
F
own, Hel - lo! hel - lo! hel - lo! there own........ ....
fz

A HOT TIME IN THE OLD TOWN

Words by JOE HAYDEN
Music by THEO. A. METZ

Em
G
know - ded ev - 'ry bo - dy, and dey all know - ded you, And you've
Miss Jo - han - na Beas - ly she am dressed all in red, I just
D7
G
got a rab - bits foot to keep a - way de hoo - do;
hugged her and I kissed her and to me than she said:
When you hear that the preach-ing does be - gin,
Please oh, please, oh, do not let me fall,

Em
Bend down low for to drive a - way your sin and when you
You're all mine and I love you best of all, and you must
G
gets re - lig - ion, You want to shout and sing, there'll be a
be my man, Or I'll have no man at all, there'll be a
D7
G
Em
hot time in the old town to - night, my ba - by.
hot time in the old town to - night, my ba - by.

G
When you hear dem a bells go ding, ling
ling, All join 'round And sweet - ly you must
Em G
sing, and when the verse am through, In the cho - rus all join
D7 G
in, there'll be a hot time in the old town to - night. . . . .

HUMORESQUE

ANTONIN DVORAK

rit.
fz
dim.
pp
a tempo
rit.
cresc.
rit.
a tempo
mf
f

a tempo
dim.
poco rit.
f
fz
dim.
p
cresc.
f
cresc.
ff
rit.
dim.
a tempo
pp

rit.
a tempo
f
dim.
p
dim.
rit.
p
pp

HER EYES DON'T SHINE LIKE DIAMONDS

By DAVE MARION

C7 F7 B♭ F7
told of his sweet - heart Nell. . . . . . Then the last one to speak was
with him brought fortune and fame. . . . . . . And on his dear friends one
D7 Gm E♭ E♭7 D C7
poor lit - tle Jack, un - to his pals he did say: . . . . "I'll tell you of
night he did call, then they sat at the old fire - - side; . . . . "Are you mar-ried," Tom
F Gm7 C7 F
one who's equalled by none," and this was his sto - ry that day. . . . .
said, but Jack shook his head, "I've a sweetheart," and then he re - plied: . . . .
CHORUS.
B♭ F7 B♭ F7 B♭ B♭+
"Her eyes don't shine like dia - - - - monds, she has no gold - - en

E♭ G7 Cm G7 Cm
hair, ... I know she loves me dear - ly, ... Then
F7 B♭ F7 B♭ F7
what more need I care, ... With a smile she al - - ways
B♭ G7 Cm E♭
greets me, . . . From her I ne'er will part, ... For, lads, I
Edim7 B♭/F G♭7 B♭/F F7 B♭
love my moth - er, And she's my sweet - - - heart." . . .

I DON'T WANT TO PLAY IN YOUR YARD

Words by PHILIP WINGATE
Music by H. W. PETRIE

D7 G7 C7 F Dm A7
f
Lit - tle sun bon - nets tied on each pret - ty head. When school was o - ver
Friends all thro' life to be, they love each oth - er so. Soon school days pass a - way,
Dm A7 Rallen. Dm C7 F A tempo.
se - crets they'd tell, Whis-per - ing arm in arm, down by the well, ... One day a
sor - rows and bliss But love re - mem-bers yet, quar - rels and kiss, ... In sweet dreams
C7 A7 D7 G7 C7 F
quar-rel came, hot tears were shed:– "You can't play in our yard," But the oth - er said:
of childhood, we hear the cry: "You can't play in our yard," And the old re - ply:

CHORUS.
C7
F
C7
F
C7
I don't want to play in your yard, I don't like you a - ny more, You'll be sor-ry when you see me,
G7
Rallen.
C7
F
A tempo.
C7
Slid - ing down our cel - lar door, You can't hol - ler down our rain-barrel, You can't climb our ap - ple
F
A7
D7
f
Gm
C7
Rallen.
F
tree,....... I don't want to play in your yard If you wont be good to me....

IN THE BAGGAGE COACH AHEAD

Words and Music by
GUSSIE L. DAVIS

F7
one be - gan cry - ing just then, As though its poor heart would
sent them this sweet lit - tle babe, Their young hap - py lives were
B♭m
Ddim7
A♭/E♭
E7
break, ... One an - gry man said, "Make that child stop its noise, for its
blessed, . . . His heart seemed to break when he mentioned her name, and in
A♭/E♭
E♭7
A♭
E♭
Edim7
keep - ing all of us a - wake," . . . . "Put it out" said an - oth - er, "Don't
tears tried to tell them the rest, ... Ev-'ry wo - man a - rose to as -
B♭7
E♭
keep it in here, We've paid for our berths and want rest," . . . . . But
- sist with the child, There were moth - ers and wives on that train, ... And

Edim7
B♭7
nev - er a word said the man with the child, As he fon-dled it close to his
soon was the lit - tle one sleep - ing in peace, With no tho't of sor - row or
E♭
E♭7
A♭
breast, ... "Where is its moth-er go take it to her," this a
pain, ... Next morn at a sta-tion, he bade all good - bye, "God
D♭
B♭m
E♭7
la - dy then soft - ly said, ... "I wish that I could" was the
bless you," he soft - ly said, ... Each one had a sto - ry to
A♭
E7
A♭/E♭
E♭7
A♭
man's sad re - ply, "But she's dead, in the coach a - head." . . . . .
tell in their home, Of the bag - gage coach a - head." . . . . .

Eb7
REFRAIN.
Ab
Bbm
While the train rolled on - ward, A hus - band sat in tears, . . .
p
Eb7
Ebdim7 Eb7
Ab
Adim7
Think - ing of the hap-pi - ness, Of just a few short years, . . . For
Eb7
Ab
F7
Bbm
ba - by's face brings pict - ures of A cher - ished hope that's dead, . . . But
Bbm7
Ddim7
Ab/Eb
Adim7
Bbm
Eb7
Ab
ba - by's cries can't wak - en her, In the bag-gage coach a - head. . . .

I'VE BEEN WORKING ON THE RAILROAD

Bb
A7
Bb
F
Rise up so ear-ly in the morn.
Can't you hear the cap-tain shout - in',
C7
F
Bb
G7
"Di - nah, blow your horn!"
Di-nah, won't you blow,
Di - nah won't you blow,
C7
F
C
F
Di - nah won't you blow your horn?
Di - nah won't you blow
Bb
G7
C7
F
Di - nah won't you blow,
Di - nah won't you blow your horn?

C7 Gm C7
Some-one's in the kit-chen with Di - nah, Some-one's in the kit-chen I know,
F Bb F C7 F
Some-one's in the kit-chen with Di - nah, Strum-min' on the old ban - jo and sing - in',
C7 Gm C7
"Fee, fi, fid-dle-ee-i - o, Fee, fi fid-dle-ee-i - o,
F Bb F C7 F
Fee, fi, fid-dle-ee-i - o," Strum-min' on the old ban - jo.

JUST TELL THEM THAT YOU SAW ME

Words and Music by
PAUL DRESSER

B♭ C7 F7 B♭
whom I re - cog-nized, My schoolmate in a vil - lage far a - way. . . . "Is
change will do you good, Your moth-er wonders where you are to night." . . "I
F7 B♭ E♭ E♭m B♭
that you Madge," I said to her, she quick - ly turned a-way, "Don't
long to see them all a - gain, but not just yet, she said, 'Tis
E♭ C7 F7 B♭ E♭
turn a-way Madge, I am still your friend, . . Next week I'm go - ing back to see the
pride a - lone that's keep-ing me a - way . . . Just tell them not to wor - ry, for I'm
B♭ C7 F7 B♭
old folks and I thought Per-haps some message you would like to send." . . .
all-right don't you know, Tell moth-er I am com - ing home some day." . . .

CHORUS.
E♭
B♭
"Just tell them that you saw me, She said, they'll know the rest, Just
C7
F7
B♭
E♭
tell them I was look-ing well you know, . . Just whis-per if you get a chance to
B♭
C7
rit.
F7
B♭ E♭ E♭m B♭
moth-er dear, and say,— I love her as I did long, long a - go." . . .
rit.

KENTUCKY BABE

Words by RICHARD HENRY BUCK
Music by ADAM GEIBEL

D
D7
G
C
Sleep, Ken-tuck-y Babe! Sil-v'ry moon am shin-in' in de
Sleep, Ken-tuck-y Babe! Bo-gie man 'll ketch yo' sure un-
mf
p
heab-ens up a-bove, Bob-o-link am pin-in' fo' his lit-tle la-dy love,
less yo' close yo eyes, Wait-in' jes' out side de doo' to take yo' by sur-prise,
G7
G
Fm7
G
Fm7
G
G/D
D7
G7
G7♯5
p
cresc.
rit.
You is mighty luck-y, Babe of old Ken-tuck-y, Close yo' eyes in sleep.
Bes' be keepin' sha-dy, Oh, my lit-tle la-dy, Close yo' eyes in sleep.
pp
cresc.
rit.
CHORUS.
a tempo
mf
C
Fly a-way, fly a-way Kentucky Babe, fly a-way to rest,
a tempo
mf

G7
C
Fly a - way,
Lay yo' lit-tle sleep-y head on yo' mammy's breast.
Ab
C
Ab
C
C/G
G
C/G
G7
C
(Humming.)
p rall.
Um
Um
close yo' eyes in sleep.
p
p rall.
C
F
C
G
(Banjo lullaby whistle 8va or hum ad lib.)
p
C
F
C
G
C

LITTLE ANNIE ROONEY

Words and Music by
MICHAEL NOLAN

Ab Eb Ab Eb Bb7 Bb7#5
Ev' - ry eve - ning, rain or shine, I make a call twixt eight and nine, On
fire burns cheer - ful - ly and bright, As a fami - ly cir - cle round each night, We
friends de - clare I'm in a jest, Un - til the time comes will not rest, But
Eb G7 Cm F7 Bb
her who short - ly will be mine,.... Lit-tle An - nie Roon - - - ey.
form, and ev' - ry one's de - light Is lit-tle An - nie Roon - - - ey.
one who knows its val - ue best, Is lit-tle An - nie Roon - - - ey.
Eb
CHORUS.
p, 2nd time, ff
Ab Eb Ab
She's my sweet - - heart, I'm her beau;........ She's
p
Eb Cm F7 Bb Eb
my An - nie,...... I'm her Joe,.......... Soon we'll

A♭
B♭7
mar - ry,........ nev - er........ to part,........... lit - tle An - nie
E♭
B♭7
E♭
1st.
E♭
2d.
Roo - ney....... is my sweet - - heart !......... heart !........
cres.
Dance.
Dolce.
pp
B♭7
E♭
A♭
E♭dim7
E♭
F7
B♭7
E♭
B♭7
E♭
Symphony.
ff
B♭7
E♭
B♭7
E♭

THE MAN WHO BROKE THE BANK AT MONTE CARLO

Words and Music by
FRED GILBERT

Am
Am7
D7
G
Mon - te Car - lo went, just to raise my win - ter's rent; Dame
great Tri - um - phal Arch is one grand tri - um - phal march. Ob -
had - n't got a sou for a Christ-ian or a Jew; So
D7
G
For - tune smiled up - on me as she'd ne - ver done be -
served by each ob - ser - ver with the keen - ness of a
I quick - ly went to Par - is for the charms of mad' -
G♯dim7
D/A
A7
D
- fore, And I've now such lots of mon - ey I'm a gent
hawk, Im a mass of mon - ey, lin - en, silk, and starch
-moiselle, Who's the load-stone of my heart - what can I do
G♯dim7
D/A
A7
D
D7
Yes, I've now such lots of mon - ey, I'm a gent
I'm a mass of mon - ey, lin - en, silk, and starch.
When with twen - ty tongues she swears that she'll be true?

CHORUS 1st time p 2d f
G
As I walk a long the Bois Boo-long, With an in - de - pendent air; You can
D7
G
E7
hear the girls de - clare "He must be a Mill-ion - aire"; You can
Am
Am7
D7
G
G7
E7
hear them sigh, And wish to die, You can see them wink the oth - er eye At the
Am
D7
G
G
man who broke the Bank at Mon - te Car - - lo - lo
E7
Am
D7
G
B7
Em
G/D
D7
G
ff

MAPLE LEAF RAG

Music by SCOTT JOPLIN

Tempo di marcia

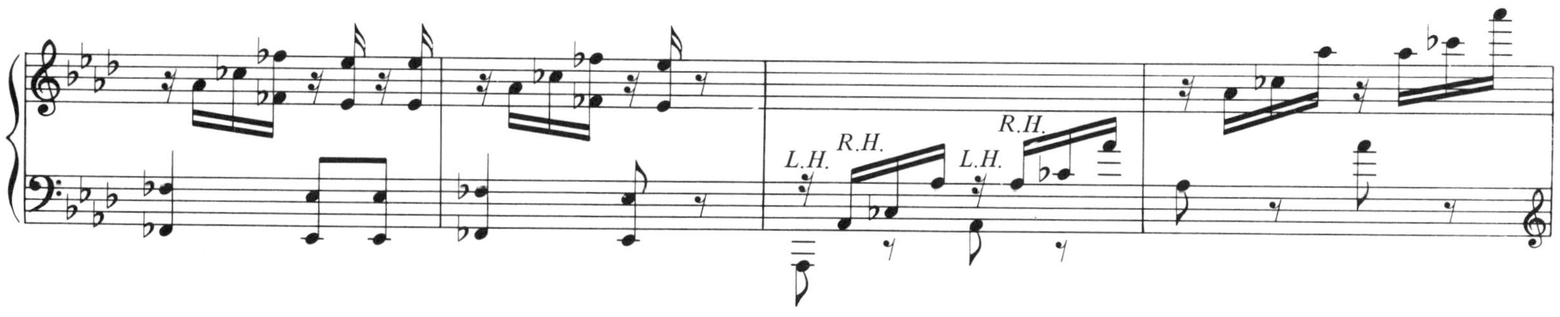

f
stacc.
1
2
f
p
L.H.
R.H.
L.H.
R.H.
mf

TRIO

MOTHER WAS A LADY

Words by EDW. B. MARKS
Music by JOS. W. STERN

C6 C♯dim7 G/D A7 D7 G
spoke to her fa-mi-liar-ly in man-ner rath-er rude; At
give me Miss! I meant no harm, pray tell me what's your name?" She
Em B7 Em
first she did not no-tice them or make the least re-ply, But
told him and he cried a-gain, "I know your bro-ther too, Why
A7 D G Gm6 A7 D D7
rit.
a tempo
one re-mark was passed that brought the tear drops to her eye, And
we've been friends for man-y years and he of-ten speaks of you, He'll
G E7 Am
fac-ing her tor-men-tor, with cheeks now burn-ing red, She
be so glad to see you, and if you'll on-ly wed, I'll
C6 C♯dim7 G/D A7 D7 G
looked a per-fect pict-ure as ap-peal-ing-ly she said.
take you to him as my wife, for I love you since you said."

Chorus.
Tempo di Valse.
Am
D7
G
"My mo - ther was a la-dy like yours you will al - low, And
p
B7
Em
A7
D
D7
you may have a sis-ter, who needs pro-tec-tion now I've
G
Am
D7
G
come to this great ci-ty to find a bro-ther dear And you
E7
Am
E7
Am
G/D
D7
rit.
G
would n't dare in-sult me Sir, If Jack were on - ly here."
rit.
E7
Am
Cm6
G/D
D7
G
f
D.S.

MY WILD IRISH ROSE

Words and Music by
CHAUNCEY OLCOTT

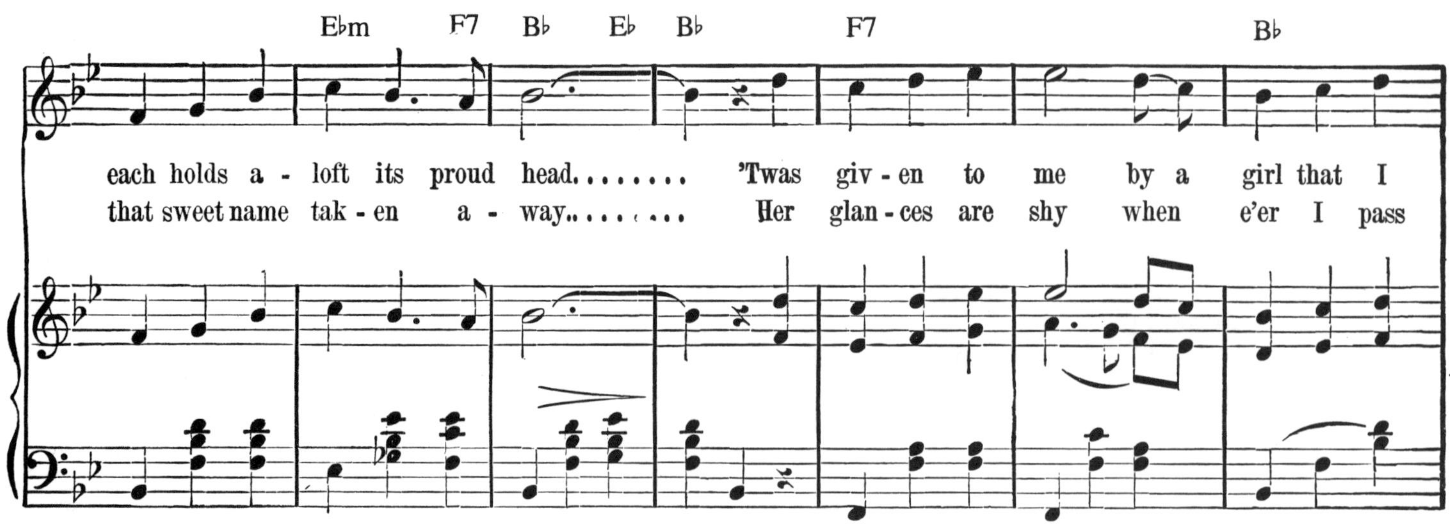
E♭m F7 B♭ E♭ B♭ F7 B♭
each holds a - loft its proud head........ 'Twas giv - en to me by a girl that I
that sweet name tak - en a - way......... Her glan - ces are shy when e'er I pass

D7 Gm C7 F7 B♭
know, Since we've met, faith I've known no re - pose,.......... She is dear - er by
by, The bow - er. where my true love grows,......... And my one wish has

B♭+ E♭ B♭ E♭m F7 B♭ E♭ B♭
far than the world's brightest star, And I call her my wild I - rish Rose..........
been that some day I may win The heart of my wild I - rish Rose.........

CHORUS.
E♭m B♭ E♭ B♭ Bdim7
My wild I - rish Rose, ... the sweet-est flow'r that grows. . . . . . . You may
p
F7 B♭ Bdim7 F7 B♭ C7 F7
search ev - 'ry-where, but none can com - pare, With my wild I - rish Rose. . . . . My
B♭ E♭m B♭ E♭ B♭ Bdim7
wild I - rish Rose, ... The dear - est flow'r that grows, ... And some
mf
F7 B♭ Bdim7 F7 B♭ E♭ B♭ C7 F7 B♭
rit.
day for my sake, she may let me take, The bloom from my wild I - rish Rose. . . . .
rit.

MUSETTA'S WALTZ

Words by GIUSEPPE GIACOSA and LUIGI ILLICA
Music by GIACOMO PUCCINI

F♯m7
E/G♯
C♯m
Amaj7
E/B
B7
tut - ta ri - cer - ca in me, ri - cer - ca in me da ca - po a
E
A
piè; ed as - sa - po - ro al - lor la bra - mo -
E7
A
sia sot - til, che da gl'oc - chi tra - spi - ra e dai pa -
F♯m7
C♯m
Bsus
B7
E
le - si vez - zi in - ten - der sa al - le oc - cul - te bel - tà.

A
E7
Co - sì l'ef - flu - vio del de - sì - o
8va
pp
cresc.
G/D
F#
Bm
tut - ta m'ag - gi - ra fe - li - ce mi fa,
mf
decresc.
E7
E7/A
A
B7
E
fe - li - ce mi fa!
E
6
pp
G#m
A
F#m7
tu che sa - i, che me - mo - ri_e ti
6

B11
B7
E
strug - gi, da me tan - to ri - fug - gi?
So ben: le angoscie tue non le vuoi
E/G♯
6
6
A
F♯m7
E/G♯
C♯m
F♯m7
dir, non le vuoi dir, so ben, ma ti
E/B
B7
E
sen - ti mo - rir!
f
p
f

OH, PROMISE ME

Words by CLEMENT SCOTT
Music by REGINALD de KOVEN

C Eb7 Ab Fm7 Eb7
p con tenerezza.
grew, those first sweet vi - o - lets of ear - ly spring, Which
p marc. la melodia.
Fm Db C7 Db C7
cresc.
come in whispers, thrill us both, and sing of love un-speak-a-ble that
cresc.
Fm Dbm Fb7 Ab/Eb Db/Eb Eb7 Ab
f rall.
is to be; Oh prom - ise me, oh prom - ise me!
f rall.
Fm7 Ab Fm7 Ab/Eb Dm7b5 Eb Eb7
p
pesante.
f

Ab
mf poco rubato.
Eb7
Oh prom - ise me, that you will take my
poco rubato.
p
Ab
Eb7/Ab
Db/Ab
Db m/Ab
hand, the most un - wor - thy in this lone - ly
Ab
Bb m
F7
Bb m
land, and let me sit be - side you, in your eyes
Db
cresc.
C
Eb7
Ab
Fm7
ff largamente e con passione.
See - ing the vis - ion of our par - a - dise, Hear - ing God's mes - sage while the
cresc.
ff

E♭7
Fm
D♭
or - gan rolls, its might - y mu - sic to our
C7
con forza.
Fm D♭ C7
Fm D♭m F♭7
ver - y souls, no love less per - fect than a life with thee; Oh
con forza.
A♭/E♭
rall.
B♭7/E♭ E♭7 A♭ Fm7/A♭ E♭7/A♭
ff
promise me, oh prom - ise me!
rall.
ff
a tempo.
dim.
A♭ Fm7/A♭ E♭7/A♭ A♭
p
rall.
pp

ON THE BANKS OF THE WABASH, FAR AWAY

Words and Music by
PAUL DRESSER

Db
Ab
times my tho'ts re - vert to scenes of child - hood, Where I
there I tried to tell her that I loved her, It was
Ab/Eb
Bb
Eb7
Ab
first re - ceived my les - sons - Na - ture's school, ... But
there I begged of her to be my bride, ... Long
C7
Fm
one thing there is miss - ing in the pict - ure, With
years have passed since I strolled thro' the church - yard, She's

B♭7
E♭7
rall.
out her face it seems so in - com - plete, ... I
sleep - ing there my an - gel Ma - ry dear, ... I
rall.
A♭
D♭
A♭
long to see my moth - er in the door - way, As she
loved her but she thought I did - 'nt mean it, Still I'd
a tempo.
A♭/E♭
B♭
E♭7
A♭
rall.
p
stood there years a - go, her boy to greet. . . . .
give my fu - ture were she on - ly here. . . . .
rall.
p

CHORUS.
mp Espressivo.
C7
Fm
D♭
F7
Oh, the moon-light's fair to-night a-long the Wa - bash, From the
mp
B♭
E♭7
fields there comes the breath of new-mown hay, ... Through the
A♭
C7
Fm
D♭
E7
syc - a-mores the can - dle lights are gleam - ing, On the
A♭/E♭
B♭
E♭7
pp
A♭
D. C.
banks of the Wa-bash, far a - way. . . . .
pp
D. C.

'O SOLE MIO

E. di CAPUA
Poem by G. CAPURRO

D7
G
re - na dop - po 'na tem - pe - sta!
Pe' ll'a - ria fre - sca pa - re già 'na
Am
G/D
D7
fe - sta Che bel - la co - sa 'na iur - na - ta' e
cresc.
G
3
so - le. Ma n'a - tu so - le
mf

D7
cchiù bel - lo, ohi - nè, 'o so - le mi - o
G Cm
sta 'nfron - te a te, 'o so -
f
G D7
- le, 'o so - le mi - o sta 'nfron - te a te,
p
G
sta 'nfron - te a te!

RED RIVER VALLEY

F
F7
B♭
G♯dim
Bdim
tak - ing the sun - shine that has
fond hopes have van - ished, for they
heart that you're break - in' and the
F/C
C7
F
bright - ened our path - way a - while.
say you are go - ing a - way.
grief that you are caus - in' me.
F
C7
Come and sit by my side if you
F
love me.
Do not hast - en to

C7
bid me a - dieu.
Just re -
F
B♭sus
B♭
mem - ber the Red Riv - er Val - ley,
G♯dim
6
Bdim
F/C
C7
and the ho - bo that loved you so
1
F
B♭
F
C7
2
F
B♭
F
true.
2. For a
3. Won't you
true.

THE ROSARY

Text by ROBERT CAMERON ROGERS
Music by ETHELBERT NEVIN

A7
Ab9
Ab7
Db
A7
Each hour a pearl, each pearl a pray'r,
To still a heart in ab-sence
Ab9
Ab7
Db9
Db+
Gb
wrung:
I tell each bead un-to the end, and there a
dolce.
Bb
F
Db
A9
p
Cross is hung!
O, mem-o-ries that bless and
ff molto tenuto
quasi arpeggio
p vibrato
dolciss.

A♭7
D♭
A9
A♭7
burn!
O, barren gain and bit - ter loss!
patetico
D♭9
sempre cresc.
D♭+
G♭
I kiss each bead, and strive at last to learn To kiss the
Gm7♭5
accel.
E♭9
D♭
Largo.
A♭7
D♭
Cross; sweet - heart! To kiss the Cross.
fff

SAY "AU REVOIR" BUT NOT "GOOD-BYE"

Words and Music by
HARRY KENNEDY

B7
E
E7
thought . . . the fu - ture lives; Our du - ty first, ... love must not
years, ... tho' past is dead. This one good - bye . . . . . must be our
A
lead, ... What might have been, ... had fate de - creed; 'Twere bet - ter
last, ... , The word is spoke, ... the die is cast; But still my
A7
D
B7
E7
far . . . . . had we not met, ... I loved you then, . . . I love you yet. . . .
heart . . . throbs wild with pain, . . . And tho' we ne'er . . . shall meet a - gain, . . .
acce - - le - - ran - - - - do.
rit. . . . .

A
E7
Say "au re - voir," . . . . . . but not "good - bye," . . . . . . Though past is
A
A7
dead, ... love cannot die, ... 'Twere bet - ter far . . . . had we not
tr
D
F7
rit. . . . .
A/E
f
B7
E7
A
Dm
A
met . . . . . I loved you then, I love you yet. . . . .
rit. . . . .
f
D.S.

SHE IS MORE TO BE PITIED THAN CENSURED

Words and Music by
WM. B. GRAY

G D A7 D A7
. . At the ve - ry next ta - ble, was seat - ed, . . . A girl who had
. . 'Twas this same way - ward girl from the Bow - 'ry, . . . Who a life of ad -
D D7 G
fal - len to shame, ... All the young fel - lows jeered at her
- ven - ture had led, ... Did the cler - gy - man jeer at her
A7 D7 G C G
weak - ness, ... 'Till they heard an old wo - man ex - claim; . . . . .
down - fall ? . . . . No, he asked for God's Mer - cy and said. . . . . .
CHORUS.
D7 G C
She is more to be pit - ied than cen - sured, . . . She is more to be
p

Cm
G
D7
G
helped than des - pised, ... She is on - ly a las - sie who ven - tured, . . On
Em
A7
D7
G
D7
life's storm - y path, ill ad - vised, ... Do not scorn her with words fierce and
G
C
B
E7
bit - ter, . . . Do not laugh at her shame and downfall, ... For a mo-ment just
A7
rall.
D7
G
stop and con - sid - er, ... That a man was the cause of it all. . . . . .
rall.

SHE MAY HAVE SEEN BETTER DAYS

Words and Music by
JAMES THORNTON

Eb
Bb
stopped for to see what the ob - ject could be, And there, on a
once some - one's joy, cast a - side like a toy, A - ban - doned, for -
told me her life, she was once a good wife, Re - spect - ed and
C7
F7
Bbdim7
Bb
door - - step, lay .... A wom - an in tears, from the
- sa - ken, un - known .... Ev'ry man stand - ing by had a
hon - ored by all; .... Her hus - band had fled Ere
Eb
Bb
G7
rall.
C7
F7
Bb Eb Ebm Bb
crowd's an - gry jeers — And then I heard some - bo - dy say: ....
tear in his eye, For some had a daugh - ter at home. ....
they were long wed, — And tears down her cheeks sad - ly fall. ....
colla voce.
rit.
CHORUS.
Eb
Bb
She may have seen better days, ... When she was in her prime; ....
mf

Gm
C7
She may have seen bet - ter days, ... Once up - on a
F7
Bb
time. .... Tho' by the way - side she fell, ...
mf
Gm
D
G7
She may yet mend her ways. .... Some poor old moth - er is
f
C7
C#dim7
Bb
Gb7
Bb/F
F7
Bb
wait - ing for her Who has seen bet - ter days. ....

SHE WAS BRED IN OLD KENTUCKY

Words by HARRY BRAISTED
Music by STANLEY CARTER

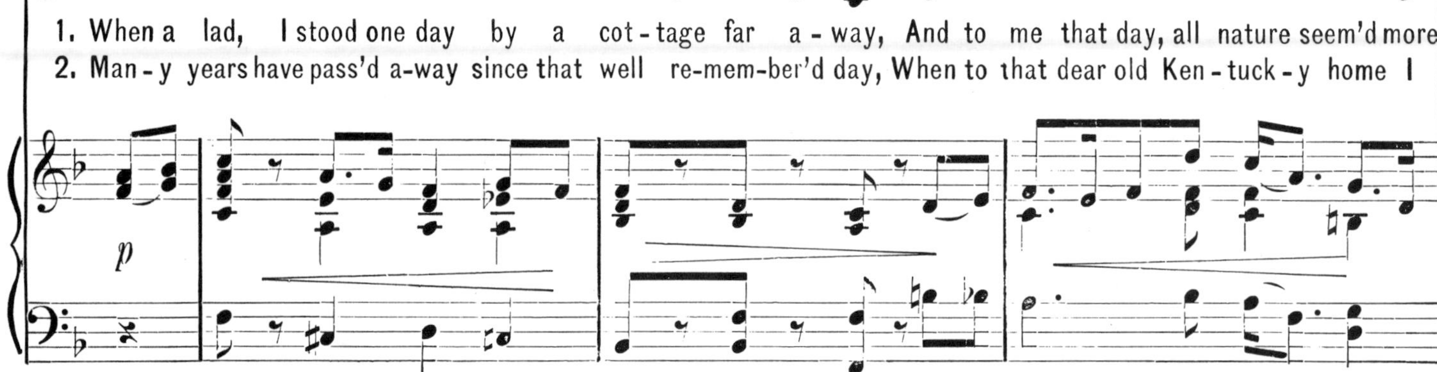

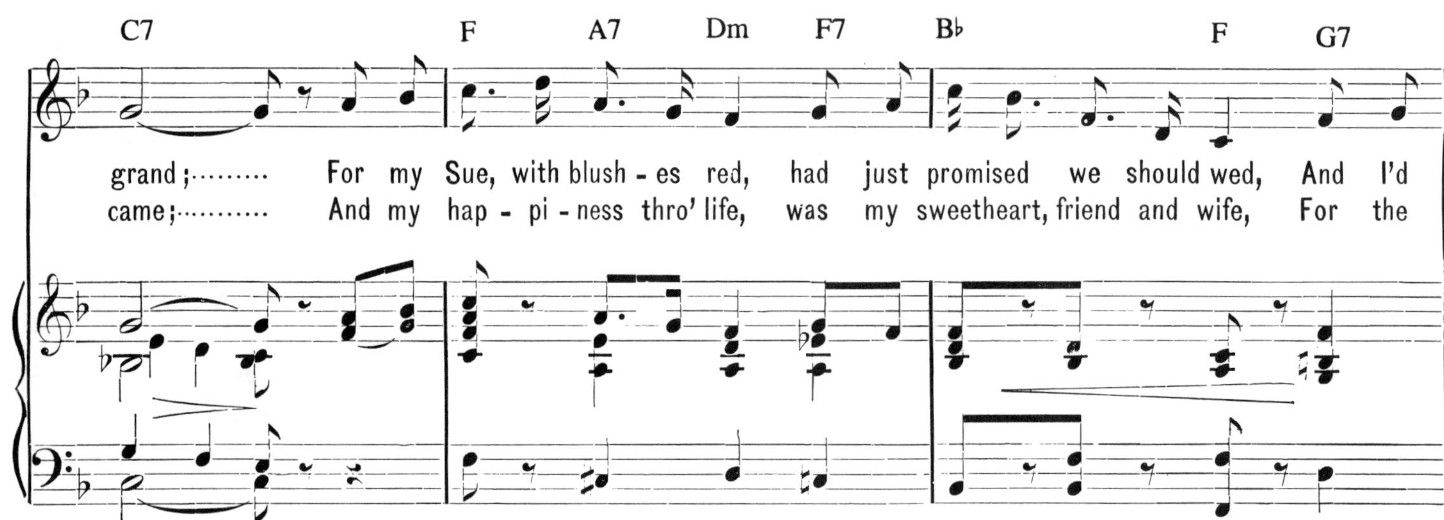

F/C G C7 F B♭ B♭m F Dm
come to ask her moth - er for her hand......... As I told the old, old tale, of a
sun - shine in her heart re-mained the same......... I am sit-ting all a-lone, in a
A7 Dm G G7 C C7
love that ne'er would fail, The grayhaired mother stroked her daughter's head,........... And I
place we've long called home, For yes -ter-day my dar-ling passed a - way;........... Tho' in
F A7 Dm F7 B♭ F G7 F/C G C7 F
fan-cied I could trace just a tear on her kind face, As she placed my sweetheart's hand in mine and said:.........
tears, I think with joy of the day when but a boy, That I took her hand and heard her mother say:..............

CHORUS.

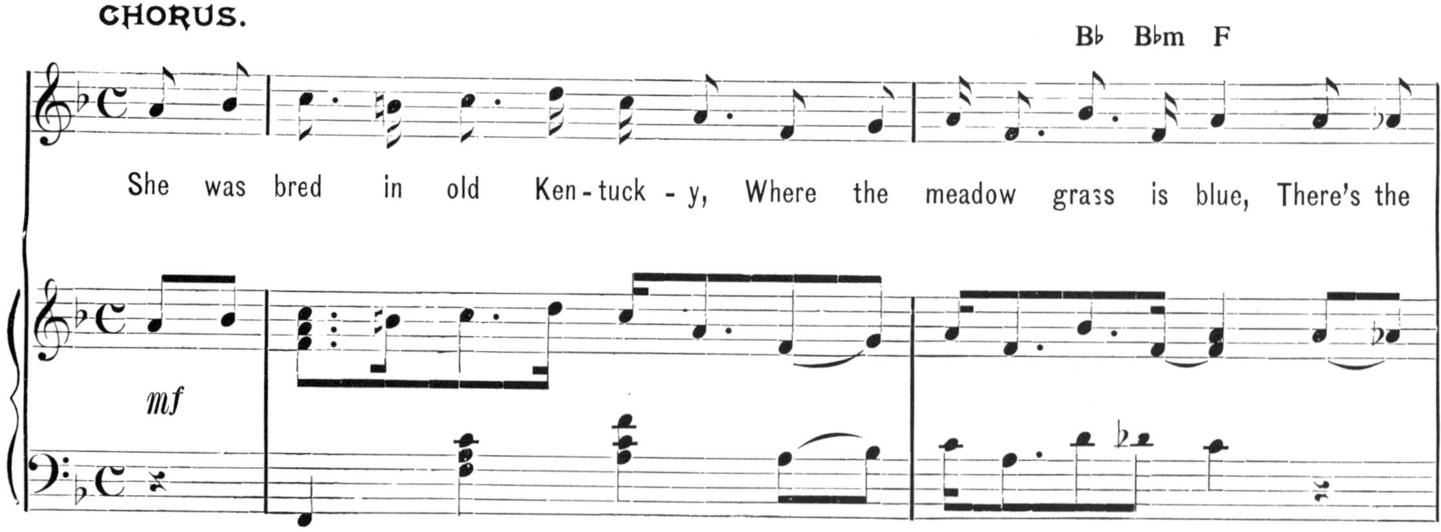
B♭ B♭m F
She was bred in old Ken-tuck - y, Where the meadow grass is blue, There's the
mf

G7 C7 F Fdim7 F F7
sun-shine of the country, in her face and man - ner too; She was bred in old Kentucky, Take her,

Gm D7 G7 Bdim7 F/C A/C♯ Dm G7 C7 F B♭ B♭m F
boy, you're might-y luck - y, When you mar - ry a girl like Sue,...............

SIDEWALKS OF NEW YORK

Words and Music by
CHAS. B. LAWLOR and JAMES W. BLAKE

A7 D D7 G D7
formed a mer - ry group; . . . . . Boys and girls to -
al - ways had the dough, ... Pret - ty Nel -
all feel just like me, ... They would part with
G C G C
geth - er, ... We would sing and waltz, ... While the "Gin - nie"
Shan - non, . . . With a dude as light as cork, ... First picked
they've got . . . . Could they but once more walk, ... With their best
G C A D7 G
played the or - gan On the side-walks of New York. . . . . .
up the waltz step On the side-walks of New York. . . . . .
girl and have a twirl, On the side-walks of New York. . . . . .

CHORUS.
D7 G C G
East side, West side, All a-round the town, ... The
C G A7 D7
tots sang "ring a ro-sie," "Lon-don Bridge is fall-ing down;" . . .
G D7 G C G
Boys and girls to-geth-er, . . . Me and Ma-mie Rorke, ...
C G C A D7 G
Tripped the light fan-tas-tic, On the side-walks of New York, ...
D.C.
D.C.

SHE'LL BE COMIN' ROUND THE MOUNTAIN

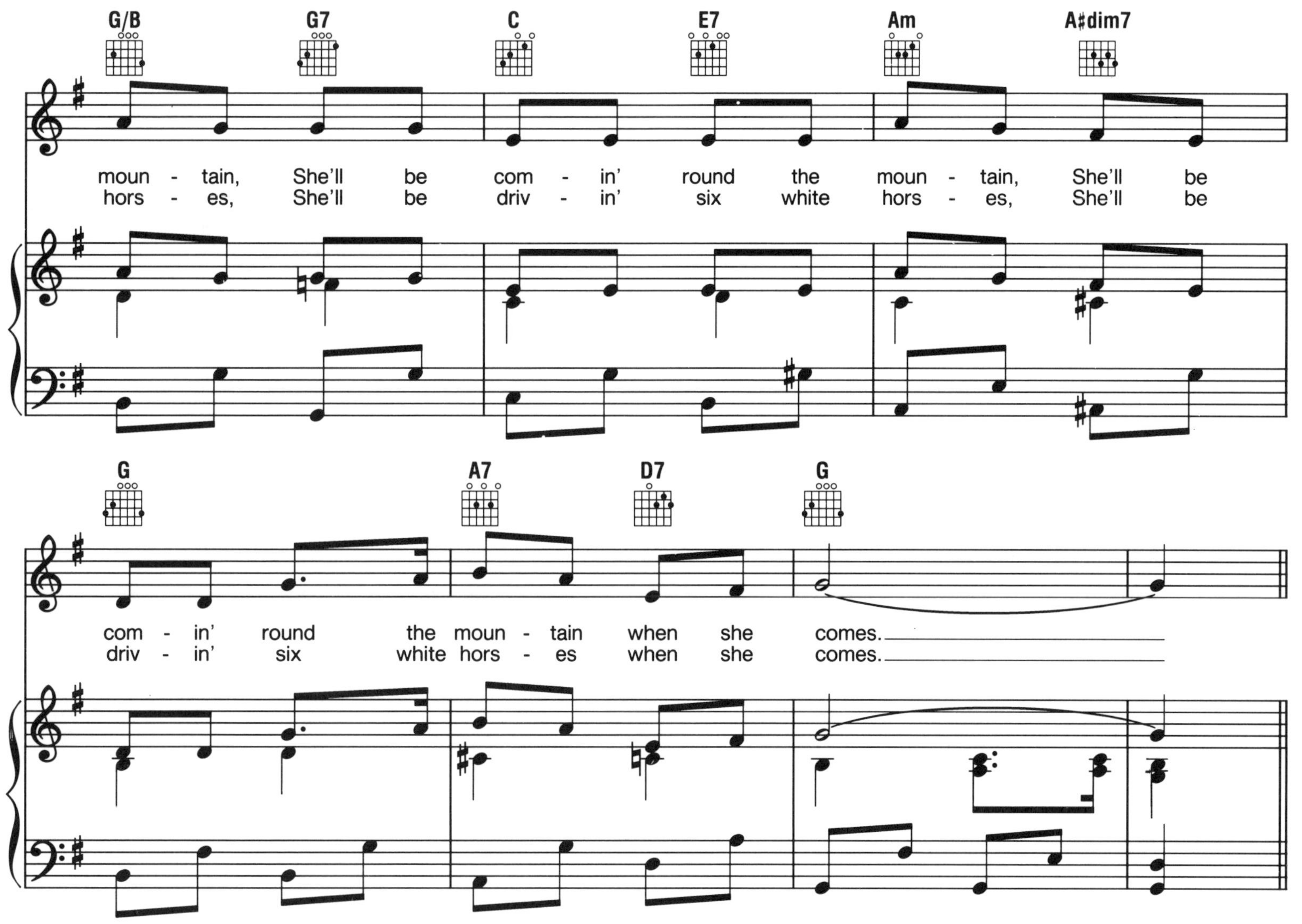

3. Oh, we'll all go to meet her when she comes,
   Oh, we'll all go to meet her when she comes,
   Oh, we'll all go to meet her,
   Oh, we'll all go to meet her,
   Oh, we'll all go to meet her when she comes.

4. We'll be singin' "Hallelujah" when she comes,
   We'll be singin' "Hallelujah" when she comes,
   We'll be singin' "Hallelujah,"
   We'll be singin' "Hallelujah,"
   We'll be singin' "Hallelujah" when she comes.

STARS AND STRIPES FOREVER

By JOHN PHILIP SOUSA

D
Dm
E
E7
1 A
A7
2 A
A7
D
A7
D
G
E/G♯
D/A
A7
D
A7
D
D7/C

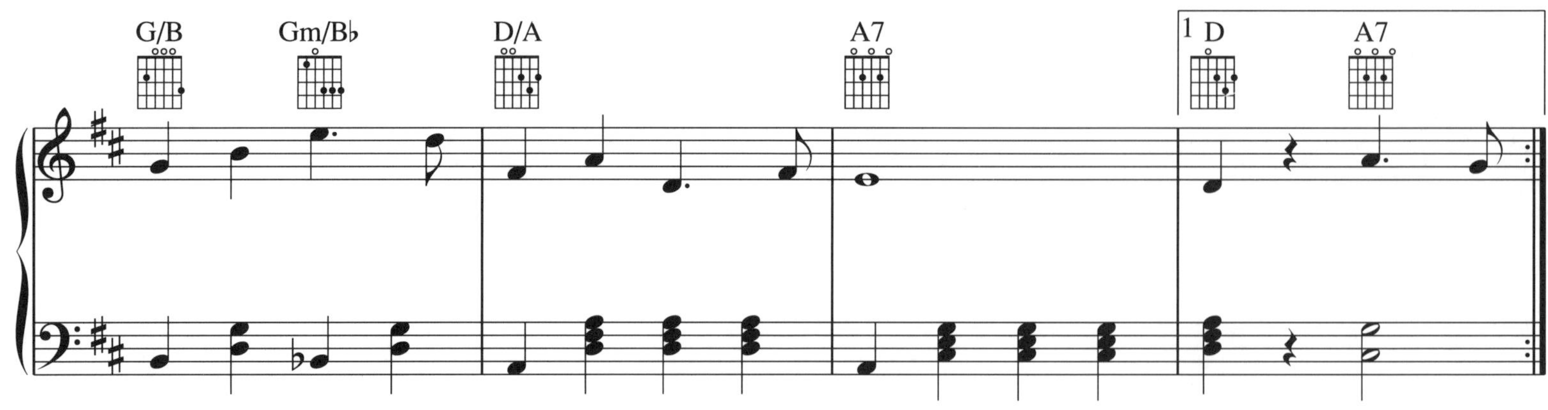
G/B
Gm/B♭
D/A
A7
1 D
A7

2 D
G
p(f)
a tempo 2nd and 3rd times

D7

G
C
D
D7
G
cresc. poco a poco
B7
Em
Cm
E♭
G

D7
To Coda
G
no chord
ff
Am
B
no chord
Cm
D
Cm6

Dm6

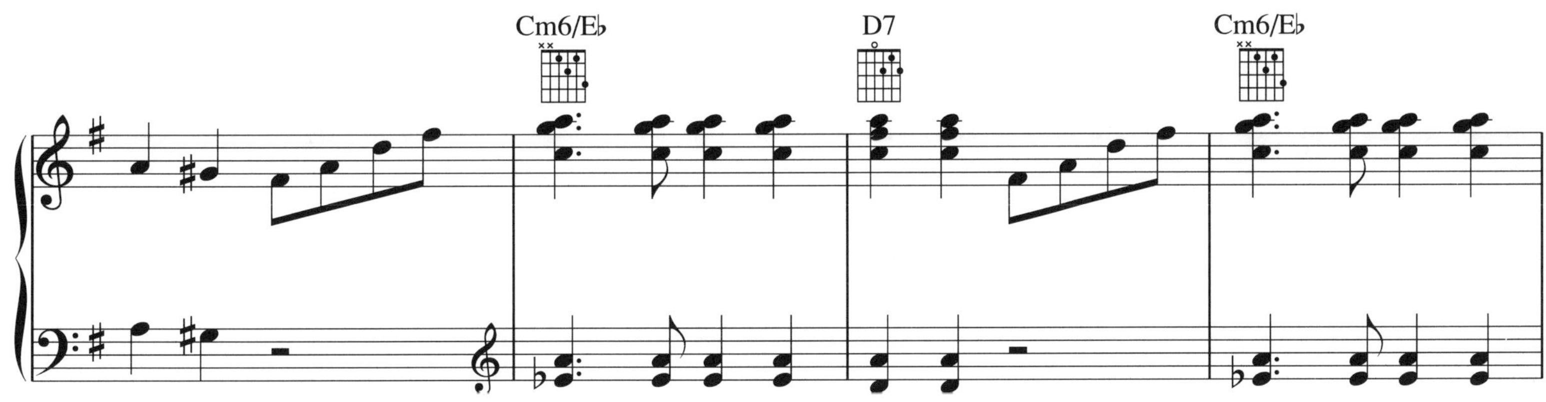
Cm6/E♭
D7
Cm6/E♭

D7
no chord
rall.

1
2
D.S. al Coda

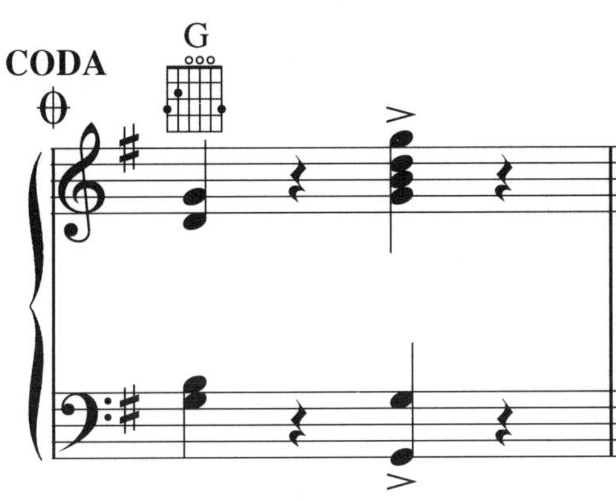
CODA
G

THE STORY OF THE ROSE

Words by "ALICE"
Music by ANDREW MACK

CHORUS. Moderato.
G
C♯dim7
D7
G
Heart of my heart, I love you, Life would be naught with - out you;
p
B7
E7
A7
Am7♭5
D7
Light of my life, my darl - - ing, I love you, I love you.
rall.
G
C♯dim7
D7
G
I can for - get you nev - - er, From you I ne'er can sev - - er,
a tempo.
B7
E7
Dm/A
Am
A7
D7
G
Say you'll be mine for - ev - er: I love you...........
dim.

B7 Em G♯dim7 Am A7 Am7/D D7
Andante.
f
E7 Dm/A Am A7 D7 G
Moderato.
B7 Em G♯dim7 Am A7 Am7/D D7
O sweet wild rose of a sum - mer day Thy love has all been in vain;........
p
G D♯dim7 Em G♯dim7 A7 Am7/D D7
Loved by a maid then cast a - way: I e - - cho thy re - frain..........
dim.

CHORUS Moderato.
G
C♯dim7
D7
G
Heart of my heart, I love you, Life would be naught with - out you:
p
B7
E7
A7
Am7♭5
D7
Light of my life, my darl - - ing, I love you, I love you.
rall.
G
C♯dim7
D7
G
I can for - get you nev - - er, From you I ne'er can sev - - er,
a tempo.
B7
E7
Dm/A
Am
A7
D7
G
Say you'll be mine for - ev - - er: I love you..........
dim.

THE STREETS OF CAIRO

By JAMES THORNTON

B7
Em
Ev - 'ry - one said she was pret - ty, She was not long in the ci - ty,
Now he's sor - ry that he met her, And he nev - er will for - get her,
All the dudes were in a flur - ry, For to catch her they did hur-ry,
Em7
C
Am6
Em/B
B7
Em
All a - lone, oh, what a pit - ty, Poor lit - tle maid
In the fu - ture he'll know bet - ter, Poor lit - tle maid,
One who caught her now is sor - ry, Poor lit - tle maid.
CHORUS.
G.
She nev - er saw the streets of Cai - ro, On the Mid - way
She nev - er saw the streets of Cai - ro, On the Mid - way
She was much fair - er far than Tril - by, Lots of more men
p 2d time f

D G
she had nev - er strayed, She nev - er saw the kutch - y, kutch - y,
she had nev - er strayed, She nev - er saw the kutch - y, kutch - y,
sor - ry will be, If they dont try to keep a - way from this
C G A7 D7 G 1. B G 2.
Poor lit - tle coun - try maid, maid. . . . . .
Poor lit - tle coun - try maid, maid. . . . . .
Poor lit - tle coun - try maid, maid. . . . . .
Em B Em B Em B7 Em B7 Em D.S.
D.S.

THE SUNSHINE OF PARADISE VALLEY

Words by WALTER H. FORD
Music by JOHN W. BRATTON

A7 D7 G
Par - a - dise Al - ley, ... But a maid - en so sweet, lives in that lit - tle
com - fort and cheer him, ... Soon the young - ster got well, and the neigh - bors all
prom - e - nade night - ly, ... We can all guess the rest, for the boy she loves
E7 Am D7
street, She's the daugh - ter of wid - ow Mac - Nal - ly, ... She has bright gold - en
tell How the daugh - ter of wid - ow Mac - Nal - ly, ... Risked her life for a
best, Will soon change her name from Mac - Nal - ly, ... Though he may change her
G Em A7 D7
hair, and the boys all de - clare She's the sunshine of Par - a - dise Al - ley. . . .
boy, and they hail her with joy, As the sunshine of Par - a - dise Al - ley. . . .
name, she'll be known just the same, As the sunshine of Par - a - dise Al - ley. . . .
CHORUS.
G Em A7 D7 G C G
Ev' - - - ry Sun - - - day down to her home we go, . . .
p 2d time f

C
G
A7
. . . All the boys and all the girls they love her
D7
G
Em
A7
D7
so, ... Al - - - - ways jol - - - - ly,
G
C
G
C
C♯dim7
G/D
heart that is true I know, ... She is the Sun-shine of
cres.
Em
A7
D7
G
1
2
G
Par - a - dise Al - - - - - - - ley. . . . . . ley. . . . . .

SWEET ROSIE O'GRADY

Words and Music by
MAUDE NUGENT

Moderato.

G D7 G Gdim7 G C♮dim7 G/D A7 D7 G

mf

G D7 G Gdim7 G

Just down a - round the cor - ner of the street where I re - side, There
I nev - er shall for get the day she prom - ised to be mine, As

p

Am A7 D7

lives the cu - test lit - tle girl that I have ev - er spied; Her
we sat tell - ing love - tales, in the gold - en sum - mer time. 'Twas

G
D7
G
Gdim7
G
name is Rose O' Gra - dy and, I don't mind tell - ing you, That
on her fin - ger that I placed a small en - gage - ment ring, While
Am
A7
D7
she's the sweet - est lit - tle Rose the gar - den ev - er grew.
in the trees, the lit - tle birds this song they seemed to sing!
rall.
CHORUS. Valse.
G
D7
G
D7
Sweet Ro - sie O' Gra - dy, My dear lit - tle
f
G
Em
A7
Rose, She's my stea - dy la - dy,

D7
G
D7
Most ev'-ry-one knows,
And when we are
G
Em
Am
B
mar-ried, How hap-py we'll be;
C6
C♯dim7
G/D
A7
I love sweet Ro-sie O' Gra-dy, And Ro-sie O'
D7
1. G
D7
2. G
D.C
Gra-dy, loves me.
me.
D.C

THE SWEETEST STORY EVER TOLD

Words and Music by
R. M. STULTS

C/G
D7
G7
C7
rit.
dim.
f
Hold me close as you were wont to do. . . . . .
Is it joy to thee when I am near? . . . .
Whis - per once a - gain the
Whis - per o'er and o'er the
F
C7
F
p
B♭
F
B♭
sto - ry old, The dear-est, sweet-est sto - ry ev - er told; Whis-per once a - gain the sto - ry
sto - ry old, The dear-est, sweet-est sto - ry ev - er told; Whis-per o'er and o'er the sto - ry
F
B♭
F
A
Dm
A
Dm
A
C7
rall.
old, ... The dear - est, sweet - est sto - ry ev - er told. . .
old, ... The dear - est, sweet - est sto - ry ev - er told. . .

F
mf Tempo di gavotte.
Tell me, do you love me?
f
Tell me soft - ly, sweet -ly, as of old! . .
C7
mf
mf
f
Tell me that you love me,
F
f C/G
rall . G7 . .
C7
For that's the sweet-est sto - ry ev - er told . . .
mf
f
rall. . .
F
mf a tempo.
Tell me, do you love me?
f F7
crescendo.
ff Bb D7 Gm
Whis-per soft - ly, sweet-ly, as of old . . .
mf
f
crescendo.
pp Bdim7 cres.
F/C dim.
G7
rall. . . . . . . C7 . . . . .
F
p
Tell me that you love me,
For that's the sweet-est sto - ry ev - er told. . .
8va.
pp
pp
rall. p
pp
p

TA-RA-RA-BOOM-DER-E

Words and Music by
HENRY J. SAYERS

You should see me out with Pa,
Prim, and most particular ;
The young men say, " Ah, there you are!"
And Pa says, " That's peculiar !"
" It's like their cheek !" I say, and so
Off again with Pa I go—
He's quite satisfied—although,
When his back's turned—well, you know-
CHORUS.—Ta-ra-ra, &c.

5 When with swells I'm out to dine,
All my hunger I resign ;
Taste the food, and sip the wine—
No such daintiness as mine!
But when I am all alone,
For shortcomings I atone!
No old frumps to stare like stone—
Chops and chicken on my own !
CHORUS.—Ta-ra-ra, &c.

6 Sometimes Pa says, with a frown,
" Soon you'll have to settle down—
Have to wear your wedding gown—
Be the strictest wife in town !"
Well, it must come by-and by—
When wed, to keep quiet I'll try ;
But till then I shall not sigh,
I shall still go in for my—
CHORUS.—Ta-ra-ra, &c.

TAKE BACK YOUR GOLD

Words by LOUIS W. PRITZKOW
Music by MONROE H. ROSENFELD

E♭7
A♭
thought them lov - ers, at their meet - ing place; Un -
she in pride and sor - row turned a - way, And
tr
F7
B♭m
- til, as I drew near, I heard the girl's sad voice en - treat The
as he sought to com - fort her, she wept and soft - ly sighed, "You'll
E♭7
A♭
one who heed - ed not her tear-stained face. "I
rue your cru - el ac - tions, Jack, some day." "Now,

Fm
C7
C
D♭7
C
Fm
on - ly ask you, Jack, to do your du - ty, that is all. You
lit - tle one, don't cry," he said "for though to-night we part, And
B♭7
E♭7
know you promised that we should be wed."
And
though an - oth - er soon will be my bride,
This
A♭
F7
B♭m
Ddim7
when he said, "You shall not want, what - ev - er may be - fall," She
gold will help you to for - get," but with a break ing heart, She
A♭/E♭
B♭7
E♭7
A♭
spurned the gold he of - fered her and said:
scorned his gift and bit - ter - ly re - plied:

CHORUS.
Eb7
"Take back your gold, for gold can nev-er buy me; Take back your bribe, and
p
Ab
Ab7
F7
Bbm
promise you'll be true; Give me the love, the love that you'd de-ny me;
Ddim7
Ab/Eb
Bb
Eb7
Ab
Make me your wife, that's all I ask of you!"
rall. - e - dim.
F7
Bbm
Ddim7
Ab/Eb
Bbm
Ab/Eb
Eb7
Ab

THOSE WEDDING BELLS SHALL NOT RING OUT

Words and Music by
MONROE H. ROSENFELD

Em A7 D7 G Gdim7
church with bell - rope in his hand;.............. As in the house of
sat and thought the man was crazed,............ The bride had not a
G C Cm G E7
wor - ship stood a young and hap - py pair.............. To pledge their
word to say, but sim - ply hung her head............ "Who is this
Am Am7♭5 G/D A7 D7 G
troth for - ev - er - more each oth - er's love to share.............. The
man?" the preacher asked, "I know him not," she said................ "Then
Em Cdim7 Em B Em Cdim7 Em Am6 Em C7 Em Am
ho - ly man then spake these words: "Be - fore you're joined for life................. Has
ring the bells," the bride - groom cried— the man knelt to en - treat—............ The

Em
C
G
Em
A7
a - ny per - son aught to say 'gainst you, as man and
sex - ton swung the chimes a - loft, the bells rang clear and
D7
G
Gdim7
G
wife?"............... Then, down the aisle there came a man with
sweet;............... But scarce their mu - sic had be - gun when
C
Cm
G
D7
G
E7
quick and ea - ger tread,.................. And, point - ing to the
forth there came a shout:.................. "Stand back! I say, they
Am
Am7♭5
G/D
D7
G
tremb - ling bride, these words he calm - ly said:..................
shall not ring, those bells shall not ring out!"...............

Chorus.
After first and second verses ff. After third verse pp.
G B7 Em C G D7 G C G B7
1. "Those wed - ding bells must not ring out, She is an - oth - er's bride, I
2. "Those wed - ding bells shall not ring out, I swear it on my life! For
3. "Those wed - ding bells shall not ring out, I swear it on my life! For
C B Em E7 A7 D7 G E7 Am
saw her at the al - tar-rail, We stood there side by side; She can - not claim an - oth - er's hand—She
we were wed-ded years a - go And she is still my wife! She shall not break her vows to me—She's
we were wed-ded years a - go And she is still my wife! She shall not break her vows to me—She's
D7 G C♯dim7 G/D C♯dim7 G/D A7 D7 G D. C.
dare not break the law's command—A guilt y wife you see her stand! Those bells shall not ring out."
mine through all e - ter - ni - ty—She's mine till death shall set her free—Those bells shall not ring out!"
mine through all e - ter - ni - ty—She's mine till death shall set her free—Those bells shall not ring out!"
D. C.
rall.

Molto agitato.
Em
Am6
B
Am6
B
3. A shriek of woe— a glit·'ring blade—a lurch— a flash— a dart— And,
ff
Em
Am6
B
Am6
B
G♮dim7
A
piu lento.
D7
G
like the lightning's stroke, the blade had reach'd her trembling heart. "You've kill'd his bride—oh God!" they cried! He
f
piu lento.
Em
Am
B
C6
C♮dim7
A7
D
swung the gleaming knife, And pierc'd his own heart as he gasp'd: "Nay, not his bride— my wife!" Two
cres.
pp
ffz
ffz
p

G
Gdim7
G
C
Cm
G
forms lay cold with - in the aisle, the hus - band and the bride,............ As
Gdim7
G
Em
A7
D7
once in life he claim'd they stood in wed - lock, side by side;............... His
G
Gdim7
G
C
Cm
G
vow was kept, the bells had ceased, and with his dy - ing breath,........... These
E7
Am
Am7♭5
G/D
D7
G
D
G
Chorus, D. C. al
words once more he mur - mur'd ere his lips were closed in death:...............
Chorus, D. C. al

THROW HIM DOWN McCLOSKEY

Words and Music by
J. W. KELLY

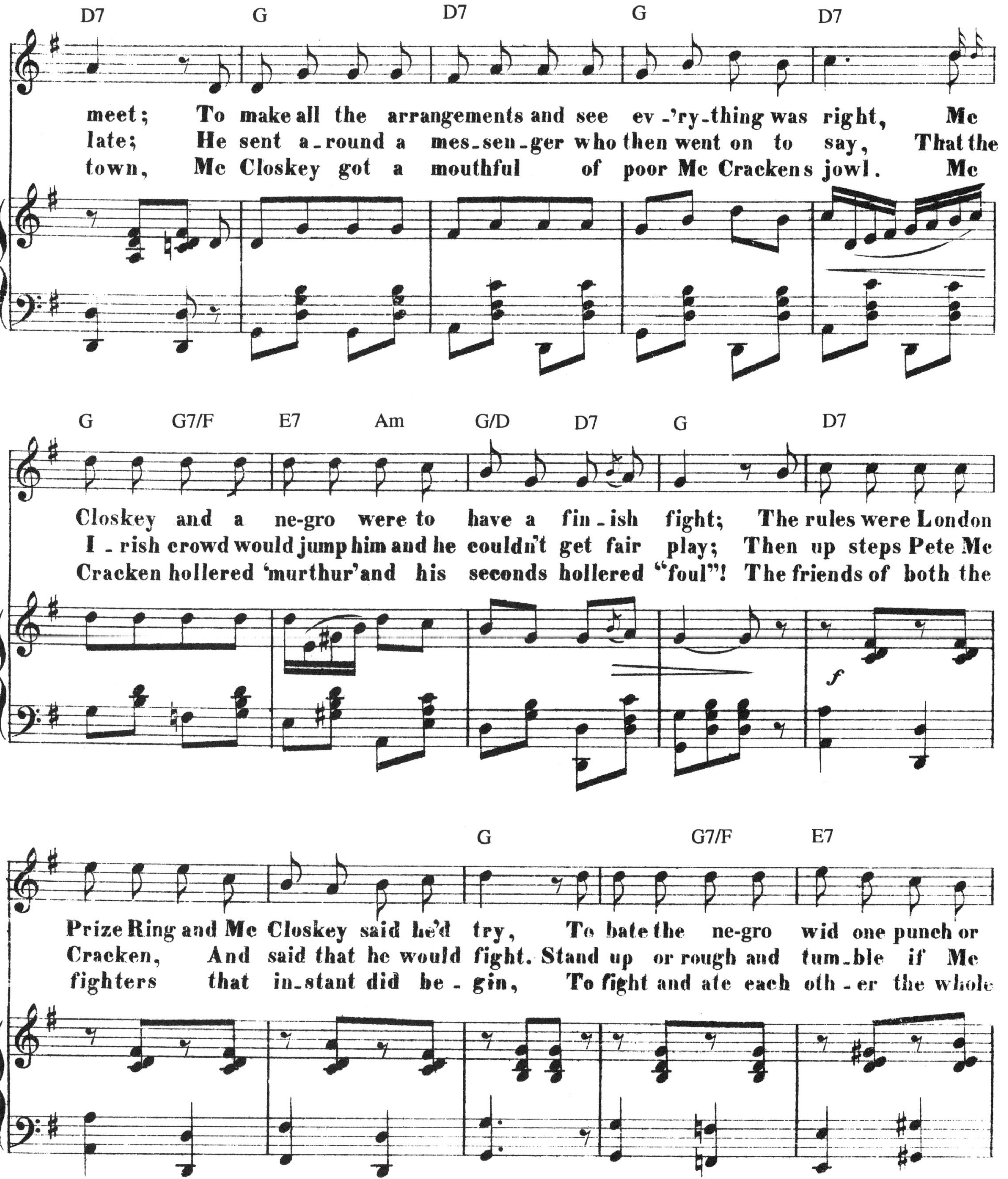
D7 G D7 G D7
meet; To make all the arrangements and see ev-'ry-thing was right, Mc
late; He sent a-round a mes-sen-ger who then went on to say, That the
town, Mc Closkey got a mouthful of poor Mc Crackens jowl. Mc
G G7/F E7 Am G/D D7 G D7
Closkey and a ne-gro were to have a fin-ish fight; The rules were London
I-rish crowd would jump him and he couldn't get fair play; Then up steps Pete Mc
Cracken hollered 'murthur' and his seconds hollered "foul"! The friends of both the
G G7/F E7
Prize Ring and Mc Closkey said he'd try, To bate the ne-gro wid one punch or
Cracken, And said that he would fight. Stand up or rough and tum-ble if Mc
fighters that in-stant did be-gin, To fight and ate each oth-er the whole

Am A7 D G D7 G E7
in the ring he'd die; The odds were on Mc Closkey tho the bet-ting it was
Closkey did n't bite? Mc Closkey says I'll go you, then the sec-onds got in
par-ty start-ed in, You couldn't tell the dif-'rence in the fighters if you'd
Am D7 G D7 G G♯dim7 Am G/D D7 G
rit.
a tempo.
small, 'Twas on Mc Closkey ten to one, On the ne-gro, none at all.
place, And the fighters started in to dec - o - rate each oth-ers face
try, Mc Cracken lost his up-per lip, Mc Closkey lost an eye.
colla voce.
a tempo.
C D7 G
CHORUS.
"Throw him down Mc Closkey," was to be the bat - tle cry,
f

E7
Am
A7
D7
G
Throw him down Mc Closkey, you can lick him if you try, And fu-ture gen-e-
-ra-tions, with wonder and de-light, Will read on his-t'ry's pages of the
great Mc Closkey fight.....
(lively.)
f
ff

TO A WILD ROSE

EDWARD MacDOWELL

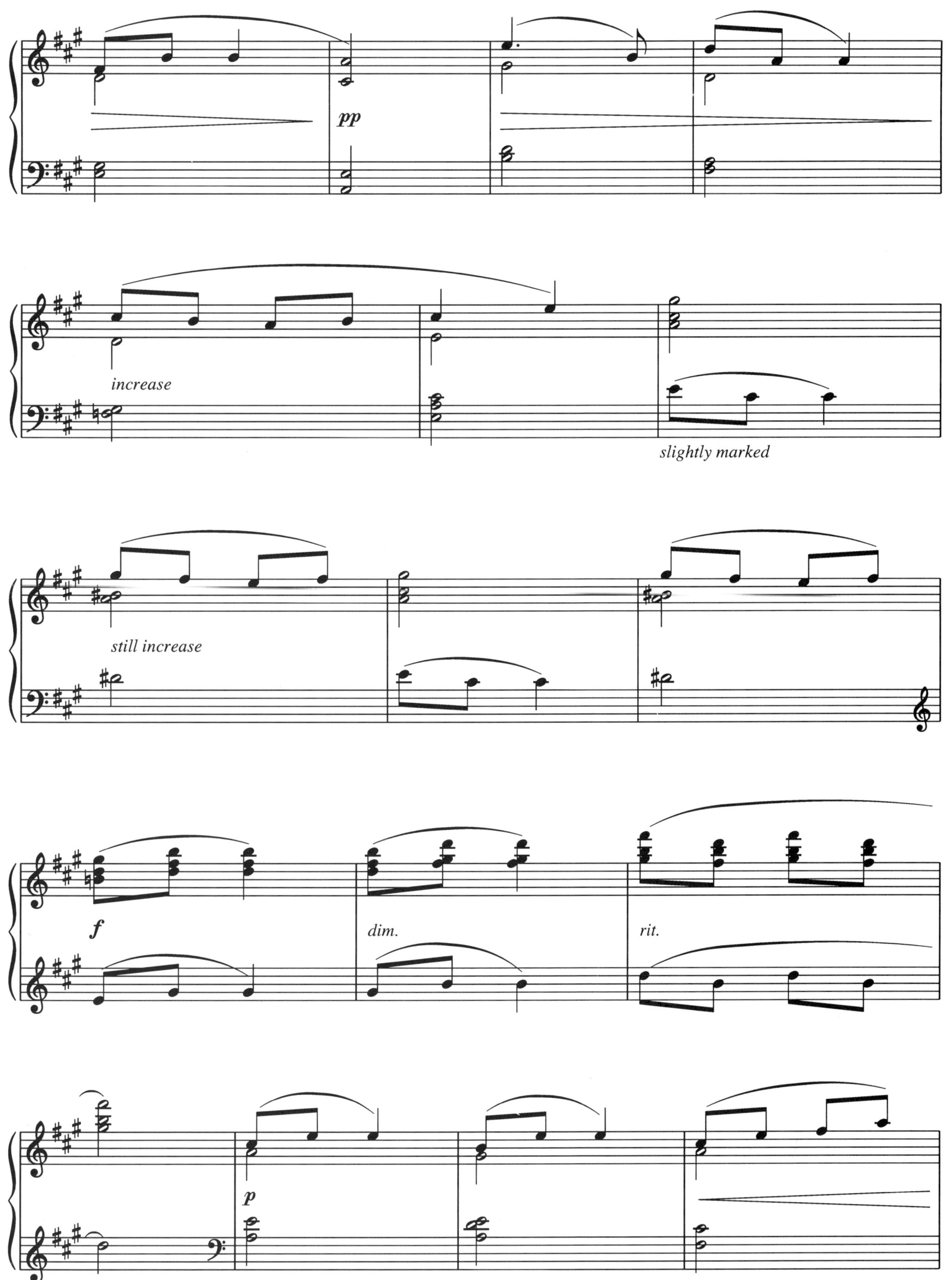
pp
increase
slightly marked
still increase
f
dim.
rit.
p

p
mp
slightly marked
p
pp
ppp

WHEN THE ROLL IS CALLED UP YONDER

Words and Music by
JAMES M. BLACK

Ab/Eb
Eb7
Ab
roll is called up yon - der, I'll be there!
roll is called up yon - der, I'll be there!
When the roll is called up

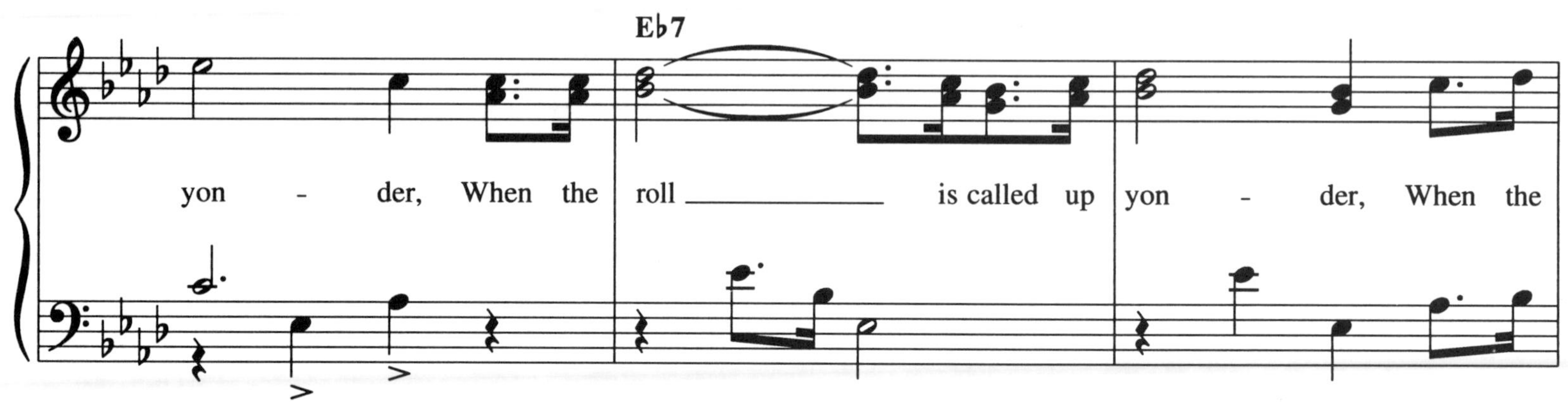
Eb7
yon - der, When the roll is called up yon - der, When the

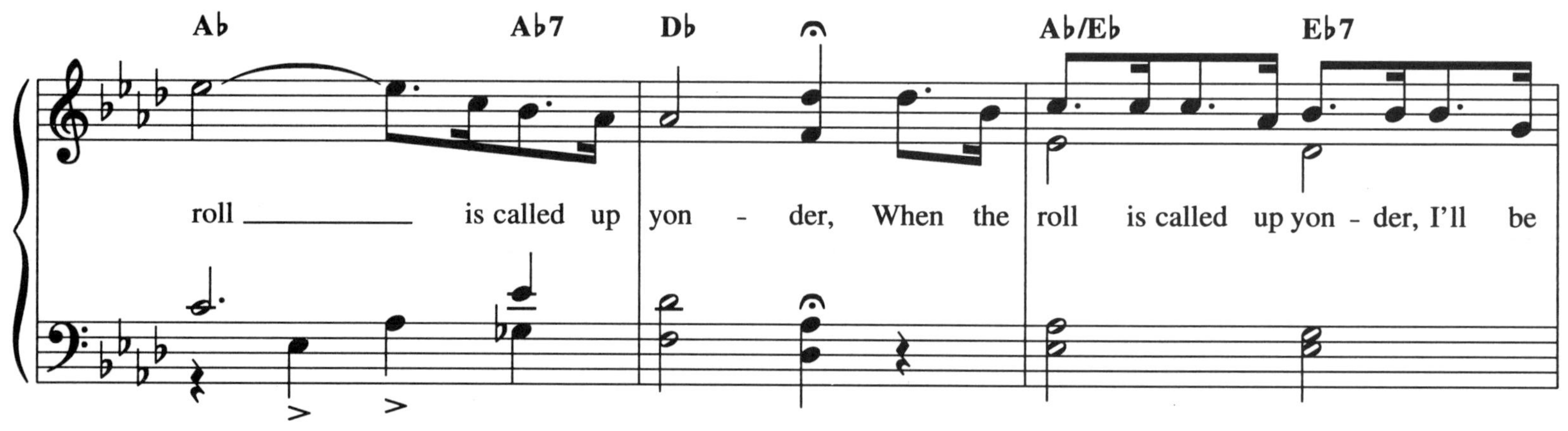
Ab
Ab7
Db
Ab/Eb
Eb7
roll is called up yon - der, When the roll is called up yon - der, I'll be

1
Ab
2
Ab
Db
Ab
there! On that there! Let us la - bor for the Mas - ter from the dawn till set - ting sun, Let us

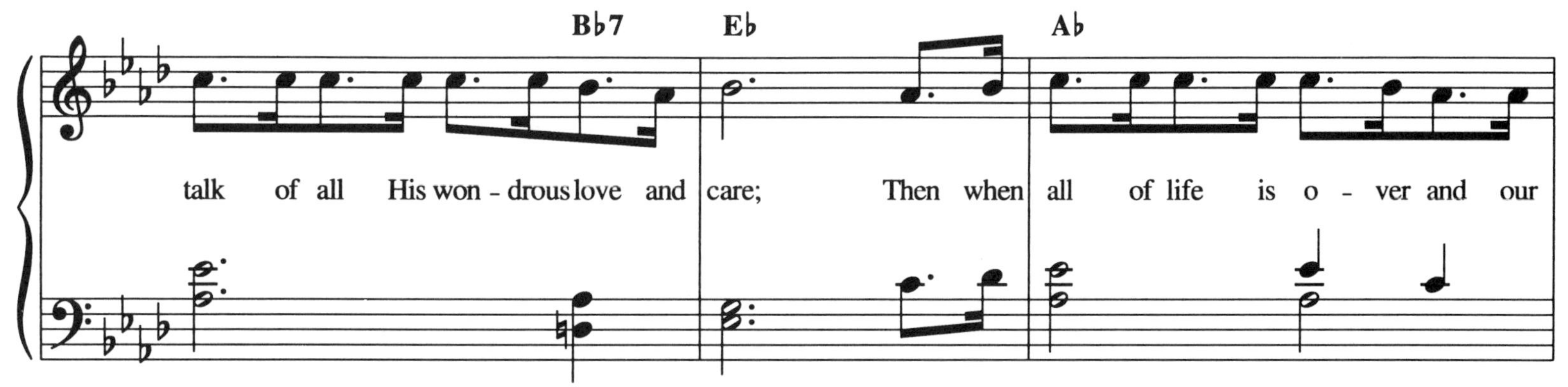
Bb7
Eb
Ab
talk of all His won - drous love and care; Then when all of life is o - ver and our

Db
Ab
Ab/Eb
Eb7
Ab
E7
N.C.
work on earth is done And the roll is called up yon - der, I'll be there! When the
rit.
f a tempo

A
E7
roll is called up yon - der, When the roll is called up yon - der, When the

A
A7
D
A/E
E7
A
roll is called up yon - der, When the roll is called up yon - der, I'll be there!

WHEN YOU WERE SWEET SIXTEEN

Words and Music by
JAMES THORNTON

F6 F♯dim7 C/G G7 C G C Cm
world had naught but joy in store for me.......... E'en though we're drift-ing down life's stream a -
to the church we wan-der'd side by side......... The love I bear for you can nev - er
G C G C G Gdim7
part,........... Your face I still can see in dream's do - main;....... I
die;.......... With - out you, I had rath - er not been born;....... And,
G C Cm G Gdim7 G D7 G D7 G7
know that it would ease my breaking heart........ To hold you in my arms just once a - gain.....
ev - en tho' we nev - er meet a - gain,........ I love you as the sun-shine loves the morn....

CHORUS.

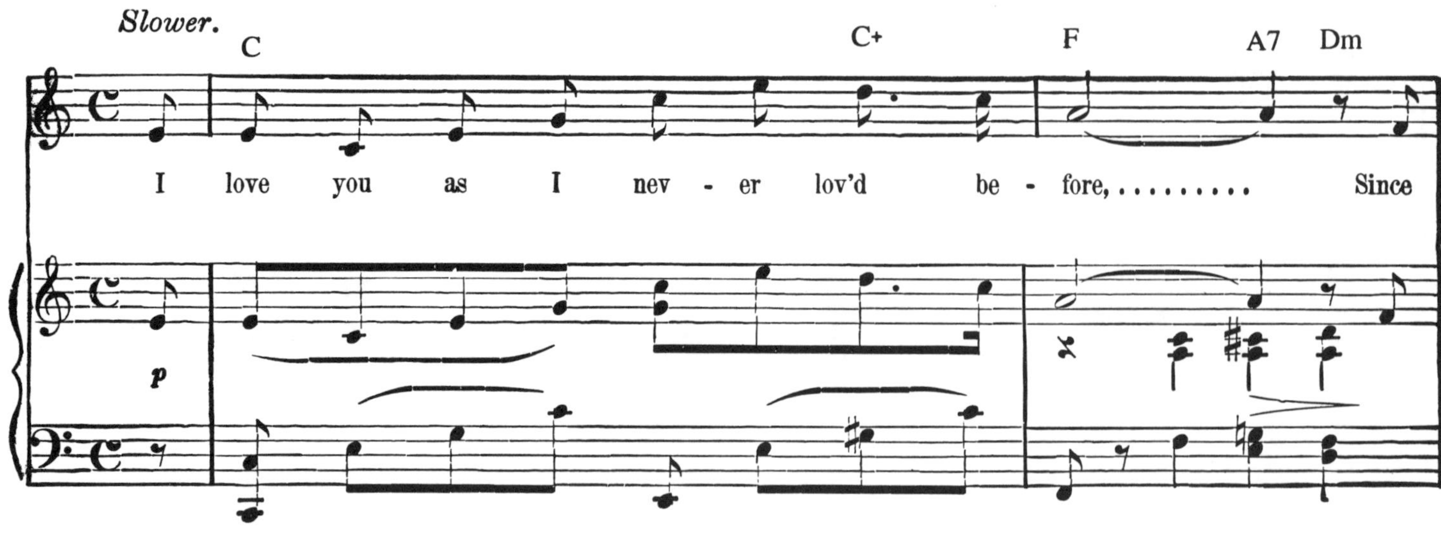
Slower.
C
C+
F
A7
Dm
I love you as I nev - er lov'd be - fore, ... Since
p

G7
C
C♯dim7
G7
C
C+
first I met you on the vil - lage green...... Come to me, or my dream of love is

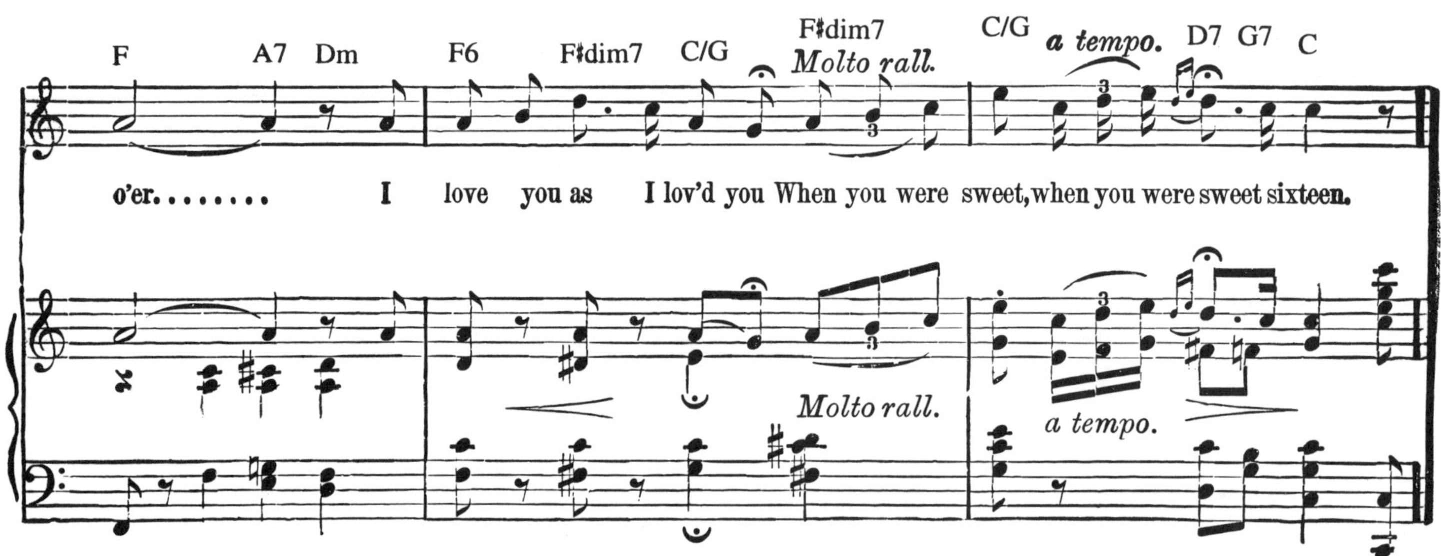
F
A7
Dm
F6
F♯dim7
C/G
F♯dim7
Molto rall.
C/G
a tempo.
D7
G7
C
o'er........ I love you as I lov'd you When you were sweet, when you were sweet sixteen.
Molto rall.
a tempo.

WHERE DID YOU GET THAT HAT?

Words and Music by
JOS. J. SULLIVAN

G D7 G C G7 F C
prop - er - ty and mon - ey. And when the will it was read out, they
out the slightest rea - son. If I go to a "chow - der club," to
said too long we'd tar - ried. So off to church we went right quick, de-
F Dm C/G G7 C
told me straight and flat; If I would have his mon - ey, I must always wear his hat!
have a jol - ly spree; There's someone in the par - ty, who is sure to shout at me:
-termind to get wed; I had not long been in there, when the parson to me said:
CHORUS.
Dm
Where did you get that hat? Where did you get that tile?

G
D7
G7
Is - n't it a nob - by one, and just the prop - er style?
C
G7
C
F
C
G7
I should like to have one just the same as that! Wher -
C
F
C
G7
C
- e'er I go they shout: *"Hel - lo! Where did you get that hat?"
D.C.

* All shout.

WHO THREW THE OVERALLS IN MRS. MURPHY'S CHOWDER

Words and Music by
GEO. L. GIEFER

Dm
F♯dim7
C/G
G7
C
on - ly for what hap-pened well it was an aw - ful shame When Mrs.
had their man - y ups and downs as we could plain-ly see And
F
C
G7
C
Cdim7
C
Mur-phy dished the chow - der out she faint - ed on the spot She
when Mrs Mur-phy she came too she 'gan to cry and pout She
F
C
D7
G
found a pair of ov - er - alls at the bot - tom of the pot Tim
had them in the wash that day and for - got to take them out Tim
C
No - lan he got rip - ping mad his eyes were bulg - ing out He
No - lan he ex - cused him-self for what he said that night So

F
F♮dim7
C/G
G7
C
jumped up-on the Pi-an-o and loud-ly he did shout.
we put mu-sic to the words and sung with all our might.
CHORUS.
Who threw the ov-er-alls in Mistress Murphy's chow-der? No bo-dy
ff
Am
D7
G7
C
G7
C
spoke so he shout-ed all the louder Its an I-rish trick that's true I can
F
C
F
C
G7
C
lick the mick that threw the ov-er-alls in Mistress Murphy's chow-der

YOU TELL ME YOUR DREAM, I'LL TELL YOU MINE

Words by SEYMOUR RICE and ALBERT H. BROWN
Music by CHAS. N. DANIELS

B♭7 E♭7 A♭ D♭
lone on the din_ing room floor; The girl of a dream had been
Ma_ry then blush_ing_ly said; Time they say brings many
grief has dis_pelled their bright dream; For Ma_ry his kind lov_ing
mf
A♭ D♭ Gm7♭5 C C7 F7
talk - ing, but re_fused with a toss of her head To tell it
chang - es, but their love no change ev_er knew And so they were
help - mate, had yes_ter_day passed a - way And in sor_row Tom
B♭m B♭7 B♭m7/E♭ E♭
all to her play - mate, un_til he coax_ing_ly said.
hap_pi_ly mar - ried, The dream of their child_hood came true.
thinks of the morn - ing, When in child_hood to her he did say.

Chorus.
Ab Abdim7 Ab Bbm F7 Bbm Bbm7b5
You had a dream, well, I had one too,
p
Eb7 Db Dbm6 Eb7
I know mine's best 'cause it was of you
Ab Abdim7 Ab Bbm F7 Bbm
Come sweet-heart tell me, now is the time
Db Ddim7 Ab/Eb F7 Bb7 Eb7 Ab
f
rit.
You tell me your dream, I'll tell you mine.

YOU'RE NOT THE ONLY PEBBLE ON THE BEACH

Words by HARRY BRAISTED
Music by STANLEY CARTER

Dm
C/G
G7
C7
sweetest thing you've seen: A young girl's heart's the strangest thing in life. Do not
man not far a - way, Was oc - cu - py - ing twice his share of seat. As she
jew-els, don't you know, In fact he grat - i - fies her ev - 'ry whim He is
F
C7
F
let her think that you are sure to of - fer her your hand, She'll
gazed at him, with in-jured look, she said, in ac - cents low, "Look
sure to call on Sun-day — thro' the week he's on the road — I
D7
Gm
like you bet - ter if you're out of reach; No
here, my man, a mor - al I will teach; Tho'
real - ly think he loves the lit - tle peach; If

Gm7
Bdim7
F/C
D7
mat - ter how you love her, give the girl to un - der - stand She's
you have paid your nick - el, there are oth - ers, don't you know, You're
he could see the rush on Mon - day nights, I think he'd know He's
G7
C7
not the on - ly peb - ble on the beach!
not the on - ly peb - ble on the beach!"
not the on - ly peb - ble on the beach!
F
CHORUS.
1. She's not the on-ly pebble on the beach! That is the sort of les-son
2."You're not the on-ly pebble on the beach! For there are oth-ers," said the
3. He's not the on-ly pebble on the beach! She has a hundred more with

4.

I was listening to a talk between two men, the other day,
The conversation ran on married life;
And I was interested as I heard one of them say
He thought that every man should have a wife.
For he said, "My friend, I'm married, and I'm happy as can be;
But dont let it go farther, I beseech!
I haven't seen my darling wife in years, 'twixt you and me,
And there are others like me on the beach!"

Chorus.

There are a lot of others on the beach!
And you can take advice from what I preach:
When on married life you start,
Take a "tip" and live apart,—
There are lots of other pebbles on the beach!

THE DECADE SERIES

The Decade Series explores the music of the 1890's to the 1980's through each era's major events and personalities. Each volume features text and photos and over 40 of the decade's top songs, so readers can see how music has acted as a mirror or a catalyst for current events and trends. Each book is arranged for piano, voice & guitar.

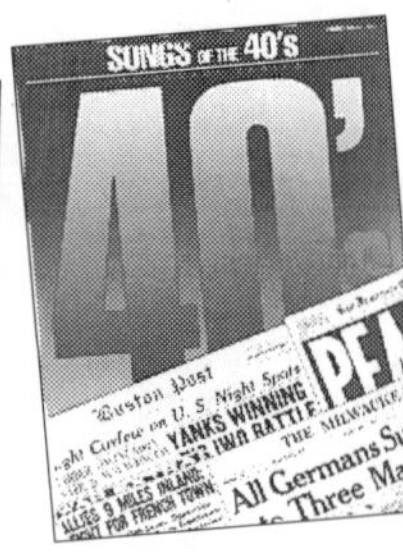

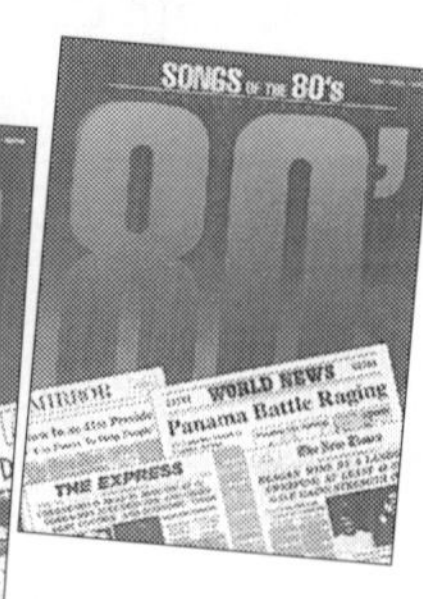

Songs Of The 1890's
Over 50 songs, including: America, The Beautiful • The Band Played On • Hello! Ma Baby • Maple Leaf Rag • My Wild Irish Rose • O Sole Mio • The Sidewalks Of New York • The Stars And Stripes Forever • Ta Ra Ra Boom De Ay • Who Threw The Overalls In Mistress Murphy's Chowder • and more.
_______00311655 ....$12.95

Songs Of The 1900s – 1900-1909
Over 50 favorites, including: Anchors Aweigh • Bill Bailey, Won't You Please Come Home • By The Light Of The Silvery Moon • Fascination • Give My Regards To Broadway • Mary's A Grand Old Name • Meet Me In St. Louis • Shine On Harvest Moon • Sweet Adeline • Take Me Out to the Ball Game • Waltzing Matilda • The Yankee Doodle Boy • You're A Grand Old Flag • and more.
_______00311656 ....$12.95

Songs Of The 1910s
Over 50 classics, including: After You've Gone • Alexander's Ragtime Band • Danny Boy • (Back Home Again) In Indiana • Let Me Call You Sweetheart • My Melancholy Baby • 'Neath The Southern Moon • Oh, You Beautiful Doll • Rock-A-Bye Your Baby With A Dixie Melody • When Irish Eyes Are Smiling • You Made Me Love You • and more.
_______00311657 ....$12.95

Songs Of The 20's
58 songs, featuring: Ain't Misbehavin' • April Showers • Baby Face • California Here I Come • Five Foot Two, Eyes Of Blue • I Can't Give You Anything But Love • Manhattan • Stardust • The Varsity Drag • Who's Sorry Now.
_______00361122 ....$14.95

Songs Of The 30's
61 songs, featuring: All Of Me • The Continental • I Can't Get Started • I'm Getting Sentimental Over You • In The Mood • The Lady Is A Tramp • Love Letters In The Sand • My Funny Valentine • Smoke Gets In Your Eyes • What A Diff'rence A Day Made.
_______00361123 ....$14.95

Songs Of The 40's
61 songs, featuring: Come Rain Or Come Shine • God Bless The Child • How High The Moon • The Last Time I Saw Paris • Moonlight In Vermont • A Nightingale Sang In Berkeley Square • A String Of Pearls • Swinging On A Star • Tuxedo Junction • You'll Never Walk Alone.
_______00361124 ....$14.95

Songs Of The 50's
59 songs, featuring: Blue Suede Shoes • Blue Velvet • Here's That Rainy Day • Love Me Tender • Misty • Rock Around The Clock • Satin Doll • Tammy • Three Coins In The Fountain • Young At Heart.
_______00361125 ....$14.95

Songs Of The 60's
60 songs, featuring: By The Time I Get To Phoenix • California Dreamin' • Can't Help Falling In Love • Downtown • Green Green Grass Of Home • Happy Together • I Want To Hold Your Hand • Love Is Blue • More • Strangers In The Night.
_______00361126 ....$14.95

Songs Of The 70's
More than 45 songs including: Don't Cry For Me Argentina • Feelings • The First Time Ever I Saw Your Face • How Deep Is Your Love • Imagine • Let It Be • Me And Bobby McGee • Piano Man • Reunited • Send In The Clowns • Sometimes When We Touch • Tomorrow • You Don't Bring Me Flowers • You Needed Me.
_______00361127 ....$14.95

Songs Of The 80's
Over 40 of this decade's biggest hits, including: Candle In The Wind • Don't Worry, Be Happy • Ebony And Ivory • Endless Love • Every Breath You Take • Flashdance... What A Feeling • Islands In The Stream • Kokomo • Memory • Sailing • Somewhere Out There • We Built This City • What's Love Got To Do With It • With Or Without You.
_______00490275 ....$14.95

MORE SONGS OF THE DECADE SERIES

Due to popular demand, we are pleased to present these new collections with even more great songs from the 1920s through 1980s. Each book features piano/vocal/guitar arrangements. Perfect for practicing musicians, educators, collectors, and music hobbyists.

More Songs Of The '20s
Over 50 songs, including: Ain't We Got Fun? • All By Myself • Bill • Carolina In The Morning • Fascinating Rhythm • The Hawaiian Wedding Song • I Want To Be Bad • I'm Just Wild About Harry • Malagueña • Nobody Knows You When You're Down And Out • Someone To Watch Over Me • Yes, Sir, That's My Baby • and more.
_______00311647 ....$14.95

More Songs of the '30s
Over 50 songs, including: All The Things You Are • Begin The Beguine • A Fine Romance • I Only Have Eyes For You • In A Sentimental Mood • Just A Gigolo • Let's Call The Whole Thing Off • The Most Beautiful Girl In The World • Mad Dogs And Englishmen • Stompin' At The Savoy • Stormy Weather • Thanks For The Memory • The Very Thought Of You • and more.
_______00311648 ....$14.95

More Songs Of The '40s
Over 60 songs, including: Bali Ha'i • Be Careful, It's My Heart • A Dream Is A Wish Your Heart Makes • Five Guys Named Moe • Is You Is, Or Is You Ain't (Ma' Baby) • The Last Time I Saw Paris • Old Devil Moon • San Antonio Rose • Some Enchanted Evening • Steppin' Out With My Baby • Take The "A" Train • Too Darn Hot • Zip-A-Dee-Doo-Dah • and more.
_______00311649 ....$14.95

More Songs Of The '50s
Over 50 songs, including: All Of You • Blueberry Hill • Chanson D'Amour • Charlie Brown • Do-Re-Mi • Hey, Good Lookin' • Hound Dog • I Could Have Danced All Night • Love And Marriage • Mack The Knife • Mona Lisa • My Favorite Things • Sixteen Tons • (Let Me Be Your) Teddy Bear • That's Amore • Yakety Yak • and more.
_______00311650 ....$14.95

More Songs Of The '60s
Over 60 songs, including: Alfie • Baby Elephant Walk • Bonanza • Born To Be Wild • Eleanor Rigby • The Impossible Dream • Leaving On A Jet Plane • Moon River • Raindrops Keep Fallin' On My Head • Ruby, Don't Take Your Love To Town • Seasons In The Sun • Sweet Caroline • Tell Laura I Love Her • A Time For Us • What The World Needs Now • Wooly Bully • and more.
_______00311651 ....$14.95

More Songs Of The '70s
Over 50 songs, including: Afternoon Delight • All By Myself • American Pie • Billy, Don't Be A Hero • The Candy Man • Happy Days • I Shot The Sheriff • Long Cool Woman (In A Black Dress) • Maggie May • On Broadway • She Believes In Me • She's Always A Woman • Spiders And Snakes • Star Wars • Taxi • You've Got A Friend • and more.
_______00311652 ....$14.95

More Songs Of The '80s
Over 50 songs, including: Addicted To Love • Almost Paradise • Axel F • Call Me • Don't Know Much • Even The Nights Are Better • Footloose • Funkytown • Girls Just Want To Have Fun • The Heat Is On • Karma Chameleon • Longer • Straight Up • Take My Breath Away • Tell Her About It • We're In This Love Together • and more.
_______00311653 ....$14.95

FOR MORE INFORMATION, SEE YOUR LOCAL MUSIC DEALER, OR WRITE TO:

7777 W. BLUEMOUND RD. P.O. BOX 13819 MILWAUKEE, WI 53213

Prices, availability & contents subject to change without notice.